WALKING THROUGH

the fire

WALKING THROUGH
the fire

CINDY VIDA

Published by Cindy Vida, in association with Wild Side Publishing
PO Box 33, Ruawai 0549, New Zealand | www.wildsidepublishing.com

Cover design & text layout: Rebecca Zwitser | stircreative.co.nz
Editing: Anya McKee | connect@torncurtain.co.nz

Cataloguing in Publication Data:
Title: Walking through the Fire

ISBN: 978-0-473-52957-4 paperback
ISBN: 978-0-473-52958-1 epub

Subjects: Inspiration, Spirituality, Body Soul Spirit, Christian, Non-Fiction, New Zealand, Memoir, Autobiography, Coping with Personal Problems, Trauma.

International listing, Ingram Spark, 2020 via wildsidepublishing.com

This book is dedicated to my three amazing children.

I honour you and cherish each and every one of you.

I honour your journey.

You are important, significant and of immense value.

I celebrate you,

I treasure you,

I love you.

May you rise up and soar.

Acknowledgements

I wish to acknowledge my family and friends who have supported me in completing this book, from those who offered their holiday homes as a space to get away and write, through to those who minded the kids for me during those times.

Thank you to those who gave of their time, offering their invaluable professional skills and helping me with the technical aspects of the book. And most importantly, to the many who encouraged me to press on, I am deeply grateful to each and every one of you.

Finally, and most importantly, I wish to acknowledge the one who invited me to write my story—Lord God, this was your idea all along. We wrote it together, so thank you for breathing your life into this book, and back into me.

Reading Cindy's story is like a roller-coaster ride. Her honesty and resilience is inspiring as she holds the line and holds her faith in the face of huge personal challenges.

I personally love the way Cindy uses practical, medical and spiritual tools in the process of caring for herself and others.

Our stories are so precious, it was a privilege to read of great courage and God's great faithfulness in this incredible woman.

– Julia Grace

Cindy writes with a passion that invites you to embrace the creative. In sharing her journey, with honesty and frankness, she equips you with tools on how to walk through your valley and come through with renewed faith, your giftings and talents unleashed, and with relationships valued and healthy. Cindy's invitation is for you to be blessed and encouraged, as she shares what it took for her to lean into her faith and develop an intimate and present walk with her Heavenly Father. You may perhaps identify with aspects of her journey and the struggle may be real and present. Yet Cindy's story is one of hope, and finding her true "north" as she goes deep in her faith walk. I invite you to sit down, curl up with a cuppa and throw rug, and dive into Cindy's tale. I could not put it down. I am blessed with your friendship. Thank you for capturing your story and sharing with us all.

– T J Kirkley

'An amazing faith journey . . . I couldn't stop reading it . . . so inspiring in many ways . . . a must read for all women.'

– Nesa Prasad

dreaming

As I lay in bed one night and began to reflect on the state of my family, only one word came to mind. *Dysfunction.* All of us, my children included, were sick in one way or another. Why, when we had tried all we could, were we still struggling with so many health issues? 'Lord,' I said, 'I have been going to a psychologist for a year and a half now; I am taking antidepressants—why am I still not getting better? And why is my son's health not improving either? I need clarity,' I pleaded, 'please show me what is going on.'

Soon, I had the most incredible dream, with seven distinct 'scenes.' I knew as soon as I woke that this dream carried the answer to my prayer, and yet, I was perplexed as to what it all meant. As the weeks unfolded, however, the significance of that dream became abundantly clear. Not only did I gain the insight I longed for; it also gave me powerful tools for the days, weeks and months ahead.

SCENE 1: Motorbikes

In the first scene, I dreamed that I was going shopping to buy three motorbikes for my son. I knew, of course, that this was lavish and 'over the top,' yet as I approached the huge, high-ceilinged shop I was very sure about what I wanted. However, as the salesman showed me each motorbike one by one, it became evident that the bikes were of poor quality, so I decided not to purchase any of them.

SCENE 2: Movies

The motorbike shop then transformed into a giant movie theatre, where a massive set of dark curtains were drawn across the windows as I settled in, engrossed, watching one movie after another. I was there for hours, unaware of how much time had passed . . . until my phone rang. It was my mum, who was clearly upset. 'You've been gone for such a long time,' she said. 'I've been waiting for you. When are you coming back?' Her call snapped me out of my stupor; I apologised, and told her that I was on my way home.

SCENE 3: The Pier

From there, the scene transitioned to a pier, where I found myself pushing my oldest brother around gleefully in a wheelchair. My brother, in real life, was not disabled—but in the dream, the wheelchair was something new and different—then, trying to make him laugh, I ran him right off the pier and into the water! Now we were both treading water and laughing! My other brother was just off in the distance in the water laughing also. The overall feeling was that we were so happy together.

SCENE 4: Call to Simplicity

My dream then shifted to a room where my husband and I were having a conversation with our pastor about how we felt drawn towards living simply. Our pastor mentioned that his parents were having a meeting at his home later that day, where they would show slides from the time they spent as missionaries. 'I think it might really resonate with you,' he said, and invited us to come along.

When we turned up that evening, I was reminded of how my grandpa and grandma used to show us slideshows about their great overseas ventures. There was also a young lady there who was going to be commissioned to go to the mission field—only, to my absolute surprise, as I began to talk to her, she told me that actually, it wasn't her that was going, it was me! Of course, I was stunned. It was so unexpected. But in the dream, she told me not to worry—I was going to have to pass through some trap doors, but on each door there would be a sign telling me what to do in order to move ahead.

SCENE 5: Trap Doors

Straight away, I was on a train. When it stopped, I got off and stepped into complete darkness. I couldn't see anything. This was unknown territory I was about to enter. I felt quite overwhelmed and almost stunned—a little nervous, not knowing what was ahead. It was dark, but the young lady had told me not to worry, that I should just follow the signs to get through the trapdoors and then I'd pass through and come out the other side, into this new land.

SCENE 6: Motel Unit

The scene changed again, this time to a motel where my in-laws were also staying and each couple had their own unit. I noticed a tall, dark, handsome man, driving around outside in a car with another man. I got the feeling they were like salespeople. In my dream, I was inside my sister-in-law's unit, where I had taken a shower—and then discovered a camera in the shower! This man had set it up and made the footage public, posting it on the internet—and now, the men were looking for a way in—trying to get into our unit! My father-in-law's comment on the situation was, 'Well, at least your reputation hasn't been completely destroyed.' He said this because I was wearing my togs when I took the shower.

SCENE 7: Tea Ceremony

In the final scene of my dream, I was sitting in a very calm, still room, stripped bare except for some mats on the floor, much like a Japanese-style interior. It was so peaceful. I was sitting quietly on the floor with my legs crossed, waiting as an old woman carefully prepared me a drink of tea.

When she eventually approached me, I noticed that her face was deeply lined and her whole countenance permeated love towards me. As I looked into her face, I became completely and utterly overwhelmed by her love for me. No words were exchanged; she simply nodded and beckoned for me to take a sip of the tea she had prepared for me.

I took the bowl of tea, and saw, floating on the top, an exquisite peony flower in full bloom. It took my breath away. I marveled at the utter beauty of it, and as I brought the bowl to my lips and took just one sip, it transformed into something spiritual, permeating my entire body, nourishing my whole being and healing me completely—body, heart, soul and mind. The woman then came up behind me and placed a cloak on my shoulders. I began to weep deeply, overwhelmed by the love that I was experiencing.

When I woke from my dream, I was still weeping. My tears seemed to be coming from a place I had never tapped into before, and it was at that moment that I knew I had encountered God.

remembering

CHILDHOOD

I grew up in a family with a rich Christian heritage. My parents both came from well-known 'brethren' families within the Waikato farming community—my father's side of the family were generous-hearted people who knew how to celebrate life, work hard, and love the Lord. My dad was the youngest of four brothers and two sisters, all raised on a farm and known for their crazy antics. My uncles were full of life and charm, and always seemed to gather a crowd.

My mum was raised throughout her teenage years by her grandparents. Her grandfather, Ralph, was a devout evangelist and pioneer who worked amongst the Maori and built many churches for their communities. When he passed away, the local iwi asked the family if they could take his body and hold a traditional day of mourning, known as a tangi, for him. Being a white person, this was an unusual honour, and one that our family deeply appreciated.

I remember my mum telling me that, as a teenager, she asked her grandpa for a ride into town one Friday night to catch up with her friends. He took her to town in a white van with scriptures painted all over the side of the vehicle and a megaphone attached to the roof. As they rolled onto the main street, he began to blare out for all to hear, 'Repent, repent and be saved! Jesus Christ is Lord!' My mother told me how, at the time, she cringed, slinking down in her seat, mortified. It was many years later that I would realise just how rich my Christian heritage was, and how proud I was of such an inheritance.

My mum and dad met at a local church dance, fell in love, married and began dairy farming together. They, in turn, had three children, and I was the youngest. Several years later, my parents felt called to go to France to do mission work on the outskirts of Paris. They set up a church in the city of Reims, working alongside two amazing French women who went on to have a huge impact within the Arabic community there. Our family returned to New Zealand when I was four years old.

As a child, I had a very simple concept of who God was. I remember sitting on the couch one sunny day, looking out across the big verandah of the old white farmhouse to where my mum was raking leaves outside. I had a yearning inside of me and said, as only a four-year-old can, 'God, I want what they have. Please come into me.' At that moment I became filled with joy and remember running outside to tell my mum what I had done. It was simple, pure and heartfelt. God had met me there and my journey had begun. I found myself praying the sinner's prayer nearly every time I went to church on Sundays, just to be sure I was saved. But as I grew in understanding, my faith became grounded in the word of God.

My childhood was a happy one, and rather carefree. Growing up on the farm and spending most of my days playing outside in nature, I soon developed a wild imagination. I sang to the cows, made mud pies under big old pine trees, and played tag with my brothers in a barn with a maze of hay bales to crawl through.

When I was eight years old, I went to stay for a while at my aunty's house while my parents were away on a trip. I remember feeling very homesick as I turned off the light at night and put myself to bed. In the darkness, a vivid feeling of homesickness and loneliness crept over me. One night, however, as I was half-reclined on the bed, my head still not even on the pillow, I heard somebody call my name. I sat bolt upright and waited . . . my heart was racing! Was it my aunty? I waited, but there was only silence. It was the most surreal sound I had ever heard, like the sound of a thunderous yell and a whisper combined—something not of this world. 'You can't create that sound,' I thought, and moments later, when it had sunk in, I knew in my spirit that I had heard the voice of God and that he had called my name. My heart was pounding as I waited to hear more, but it was only my name I heard, nothing more. Stunned, I lay down and eventually went to sleep, not knowing that more was certainly to come, just not that night.

I grew into a teenager who was deeply passionate and sincere about my faith. I was outgoing and loved the crazy side of life, always egging my friends on to do outlandish things. I spent my school years in the performing arts—acting, singing and public speaking—which led me into leadership roles such as becoming head girl of my school. I was blessed to have been part of a group of Christian friends who were arty, fun and uncomplicated! These have become lifelong friends whom I still cherish.

At home, I was surrounded by a full and sociable house. My parents were very involved with an organisation called, 'Youth for Christ', and as a family, we often entertained and billeted bands that came through on tour. Of course, I 'fell in love' with each new band member that passed through town. My parents were incredibly inclusive people and extremely generous with the way they lived their lives. To this day, I am grateful that they imparted this to us, their children.

I have always been sincere in my faith, feeling as if God has been in every fibre of my being since I was a young girl. I have always felt very close to God, in the same intimate way as a tender father with a child, someone who has always had his heart inclined towards me. My parents would say I had a very compassionate heart towards the poor and needy, and those less fortunate than ourselves. At times, I exasperated them, I am sure. When I was at university, I wanted to sell my car and give the money to the poor. I remember insisting that my parents did not need this, that and the other thing. 'Why don't we just keep enough to live, and give everything else away to the poor?' I often argued.

Around that time, I received a payout from the accident compensation board. I had been playing netball at a competitive level throughout my teenage years and was part of a developmental squad which worked alongside regional players in the hope of developing them into national players. I was at my peak performance, training and playing six days a week. The accident occurred while I was playing in a tournament in the South Island of New Zealand. It was a semi-final match, and I had jumped up to tip the ball of a very tall shooter. As I landed, however, I came down on top of my opponent's shoe, rolled my ankle, and totally wrenched my knee, which locked it into a ninety-degree position. I was taken off the court in a wheelchair, and that was the end of my netball career at that level. Under the compensation scheme, I was paid out under the premise of 'loss of potential.'

My dad knew I had the money from my netball incident sitting in my account, and I think he was nervous that I might give it all away. In the meantime, he had begun to dabble in real estate— one day, as I was walking through the university campus, heading towards a lecture, I received a call. 'Cindy, it's dad. Do you want to buy a house?' he asked in a quiet voice. 'What?! No!' I replied. 'Look,' he said, 'I'm sitting in an auction right now, and an absolute bargain has come up. It's a little house, but it's a mortgagee sale, and you'd probably get it for about thirty thousand dollars. I can't bid on it, because I'm a real estate agent, but you can!'

'Dad, I don't want to buy a house,' I insisted, 'I'm twenty-one, and I am going to buy my first house with my husband! That's my plan.' I couldn't actually believe what he was asking. 'Look, Cindy,' he said, talking faster now, with urgency in his voice. 'Try not to think of it as your first home. Just think of it as an investment, just like buying a herd of cows. I'll help you, and we can renovate it together, then flick it off to make a profit.'

I thought this was crazy, but dad had a way of making me somehow believe that it was all going to be fantastic and work out brilliantly. He was a big fan of the motivational speaker Zig Ziglar; positivity was his middle name. I wasn't completely convinced, but dad could be ever so persuasive, and I trusted him. 'Okay,' I agreed, 'I'll buy the house!' As it happened, the bid my father placed for me was successful, and just like that, without ever having seen the place, I became the proud owner of my first home. My dad was relieved. The compensation money was secure. This was a win-win situation.

The house I purchased was a quaint little two-bedroom home set on a large scruffy section on the outskirts of a small city a few hour's drive from my home. It was solidly constructed, with no major issues, other than cosmetic ones. I began to 'set up home' in my female imagination, planning ways to 'dress the rooms.' After coming up with an array of creative colour schemes, I ended up painting the house a vivid terracotta colour.

Dad had a hard time trying not to squash my enthusiasm, but he also wanted to teach me about the importance of not getting emotionally attached to the property. It was a challenge for him, as he tried to make me view the place as an investment, doing it up in a way that would enhance resale value, rather than as my first sweet home.

My dad had a formula when it came to renovating . . . he liked to turn up with a chainsaw and cut a hole between two rooms to create an 'open plan.' It was 'good ole Kiwi DIY' coming out to play! After sawing out huge spaces, opening up the kitchen, dining room and lounge, he simply whacked in a set of French doors, built a deck, gave the house a lick of paint inside and out, did a quick tidy up of the yard and we were good to go! Time for resale. I grew up listening to many dinner conversations about potential investment schemes and how to improve and flick off properties. Dad was always number crunching and dreaming about the next great idea—it's no surprise, then, that the language of profit and investment, and the accompanying way of seeing things, was in my blood.

I ended up attending teacher's college in my hometown and as a young adult, began to attend a Pentecostal church during my time at university. This was a time when my faith grew, particularly in terms of the prophetic and the influence of the Holy Spirit. Four years' later, as a twenty-one-year-old, I knew I was ready to spread my wings and fly. I needed adventure—but I also sensed that I was being drawn away for a larger plan and purpose, and so I began applying for jobs all over New Zealand, literally, from the very top to the extreme south of the country—and beyond.

I even applied for a job in Papua New Guinea as a sole charge principal, a role that required the successful applicant to travel inland and then journey upstream by boat to the location of the school. 'That sounded a bit like me,' I thought. I had decided to apply for jobs anywhere except for my hometown of Hamilton, or Auckland, since Auckland had a reputation as being an unfriendly and arrogant city for anyone who came from outside.

Even with my gleaming resume and extensive array of applications in place, however, I was not getting any interviews. It wasn't until further down the track that I knew why. The doors had been firmly shut because God only had one place in mind for me to be, and I only found out when a letter arrived in the post. 'We are pleased to invite you to an interview at Waimauku Primary School,' it said. 'Waimauku?' I thought, 'where the heck is that?!'

Pulling out a map of New Zealand, I found it—a little township on the coast, just above the shaded area that was officially designated as Auckland! 'My goodness, that's a bit close, don't you think, God?' I asked. 'I mean, I did say anywhere but Auckland, didn't I?' I looked at the map again and smiled. 'Well, I suppose it is not officially Auckland, even though I will have to drive through Auckland every time I go back to visit my family,' I conceded.

I look back now and think, how clever he is. God obviously had plans for me in Auckland but knew he couldn't get me there unless he eased me into the fringes first. 'Very funny,' I thought. I drove to the interview through the 'spaghetti junction' on the motorway, holding my breath and wondering what the heck I, a country girl, was getting myself in for. Everyone knew me in Hamilton—there, in the northern suburbs of Auckland, no-one knew me. Underlying all of the unknowns, I sensed God's purpose over my life as I drove into totally foreign and new territory. Soon, I had a new job, and with that, came a new home, new friends, new church, new *everything*—and yet somehow, I just knew it was right.

I eventually settled in a little seaside town just twenty minutes' drive from my first teaching job. I drove around in an old Blue

Morris 1000, which I loved. With no heating, it was freezing to drive, so I draped my nana's old crocheted rug over my shoulders, and off I set. The car had no radio, but I carried a large old ghetto blaster requiring eight DD batteries in the back seat (most cost ineffective) and blasted it out as loud as I could. I also bought the cutest black and white kitten; I called her Jazz, and she travelled in the car with me everywhere. As my companion, she would sit on my shoulder as I drove. Life was good. I was on an adventure and the 'crazy' in me had come out to play!

My home was a little blue shack, with a spectacular view that made the one-hundred and twenty-four step climb from the front door to the street above totally worth it. From that home, I could look out across the ocean and right down the beach—as far as the eye could see . . . freedom! The 'shack' sat snuggly into the side of the hill, and with no neighbours or flatmates, I was on my own and it was perfect. At night when my creative surges rose I would paint, and throughout the day, I taught children at the local school.

Some mornings my car would refuse to start, and then I would hitchhike to catch a ride to work. With only one road leading in the direction of the school, someone would eventually notice me. Sure enough, it was invariably a parent dropping her child off to the same school who would stop and offer to take me. I remember one little girl sprinting away from the car, absolutely bursting to tell her friends who she had picked up hitchhiking on their way to school that day . . . the teacher!

I quickly moved on from regular classroom teaching, to taking a position as the special needs teacher at a satellite unit for the area. What joy and challenges all rolled into one! Those kids made my heart soar. I was so happy and content working alongside them;

we had so much fun together and it was the perfect environment for my creative slant to be utilised. Once, I transformed the classroom into a forest; other times it became an underwater world. I poured my heart and soul into those kids. I'm not sure how much I taught them, but I do know that they taught me that simple pleasures are to be cherished, that what the world deems success is really not success at all, and that to love and be loved is a precious gift that we can impart to one another. I always felt that they were the blessed ones, that somehow they had an open portal to heaven, a sort of communion with the Lord. They seemed to sense his pleasure and delight and love for them, carrying a simple yet overwhelming level of joy and a shining countenance. 'What were we missing?' I wondered. 'We strive for so much, and yet in these children, beauty is found in simply being. Being themselves.'

There is no end to the stories I could tell from those years. One lunch-hour, a call was put through to me from the police. They were concerned, because they had received a distress-call from the special needs unit, and then the phone had been hung up. I thanked the police and raced outside to see what might have happened. There in the playground, two of my students stood, looking at me with big guilty eyes. 'What's going on, boys?' I asked them. 'Is everything okay? Did one of you use the phone in my office?'

One of the boys, a lovely, blonde-haired, blue-eyed ten-year old tried to answer. 'Yes,' he replied, speaking very slowly and deliberately as he began to walk into the office as if to re-enact what he had done. 'I . . . picked . . . up . . . the . . . phone.' 'Oh,' I said, 'and what number did you call?' '1 . . . 1 . . . 1' he said slowly. 'Okay,' I smiled, 'and what did you say?' 'I said . . . "help! Come quickly . . . someone . . . is . . . hitting . . . me . . . on . . . the head!" he replied. "And then . . . I hung up,'" he said. I laughed, thankful that I had a well-developed sense of humour!

AN ENCOUNTER

Being away from my family for the first time in my life, I began, around this time, to wonder about the things I had always believed. Was God really *real*? Did I just believe in him because that was all I had known and all I was taught? What about the other faiths? Who are we to say that one God is the real deal and others are not? I wanted to know for sure; most importantly, I wanted my faith to be authentic. I did not want to sit on the fence. I wanted to either be in or out, and if I was in, I was going to be wholeheartedly in. I wanted to own my faith as *my own*, not as my family's faith. I had studied the five major religions of the world as part of a university paper, and as I contemplated, I found I had a lot of questions that needed to be answered.

I had begun attending a small local church nearby, but the services felt dry and boring. I remember waking up one sunny Sunday morning and saying, 'Okay Lord, I know you can speak to me wherever I am as long as my heart is open to you, so I am going to go to church with an expectant heart today.' Puttering off down the road in my little Morris, I arrived at the church and slipped into the back row. As the service began, my thoughts took me back to the time when I was a little girl and God spoke to me. 'How profound,' I thought, 'that God had chosen to speak to me.' I was perplexed. 'God,' I asked, 'If you are the God of the universe and you wanted to speak to me, why, of all the things you could have said, did you just speak my name? Why? What good is that to me? Why couldn't you have said something really profound to me, like, "This is what you're going to do with your life . . ?" God, if that really was you, then why did you waste your breath just saying my name? What was the point of that?'

As I was asking the question of God, a woman got up at the front of the church and began to speak. 'I feel like this is a scripture for someone here in this room today,' she began to say, and then she read the words of Isaiah 43:1-4:

> But this is what the Lord says,
> he who created you . . . he who formed you . . .
> 'Fear not, *for I have called you by name.* Child, you are mine!
> When you pass through the waters, I will be with you,
> and when you pass through the rivers, they will not
> sweep over you.
> When you walk through the fire you will not be burned,
> the flames will not set you ablaze.
> For I am the Lord your God, the Holy One of Israel,
> your Saviour.
> I give Egypt for your ransom, Cush and Seba in your stead
> since you are precious and honored in my sight,
> and because I love you.'

Wow! God had answered. He had completed the sentence he had started with me when I was just eight years old. As I was asking him, he was simultaneously answering me! I was stunned—and deeply moved. 'Cindy . . . I have called you by name . . . child, you are mine.'

It was significant to me that he had answered me through the word of God, the Bible. This God I trusted was the God of Israel—not Buddha, or Allah, or any other God—and He had told me that he loved me, that I was precious to him and that he was going to be with me and walk with me all the days of my life.

That was good enough for me. My faith was solidified by that encounter; from that point on, there was no turning back. God had drawn me to himself and called me out. It was the Lord's promise to me that he was real. Still, I thought about the words in that passage. 'What do you mean, troubled times?' I wondered. 'I haven't had troubled times—I'm having a great time. It's great that you are going to be with me, but Lord, I don't care too much about the the flames and the waters and the drowning!' I chose to dismiss all of that, as only a young twenty-one year old can, and carried on.

What I did not know, was that the promise that God would never leave my side was to become a scripture I would cling to with all that I had, in the years that lay ahead of me.

FALLING IN LOVE

I had never really been one to pursue boys—I always thought that was their job. I was going to get on with my life, and if they liked what they saw in me, they had better jolly well get on-board with me in the journey. After my epiphany, however, I realised that I needed to get into a larger church to meet other people, to stretch and grow. The church closest to me that fit the bill was just within the shaded official Auckland zone. 'What the heck,' I thought. 'Let's give this place a try.' I turned up to the Sunday service, thought it was friendly enough, then grabbed an information brochure and headed home afterwards.

Flicking through the brochure later that day, I noticed that there was a young adults group being held on Tuesday night, so I wrote down the address and decided to go along, unannounced. Walking down the long driveway, I heard laughter coming from the converted garage. 'That must be it,' I thought, and as I opened the sliding door, I did what I always do when I am completely nervous: I clicked into 'Miss Overconfident' mode. 'Hi!' I said. 'Is this the young adults' bible study?'

Everyone stared at me, a little taken aback, and one young man was particularly amused by my entrance. Years later he told me exactly what I was wearing that night—a pair of jeans, a white linen shirt, and a black beret. He recalled how half-way through the evening, with my newfound passion for my faith, I became frustrated and blurted out, 'Are we going to open our bibles? This is a bible study after all, isn't it?'

I met Jimmy that night, and soon, I fell in love. Jimmy and I became inseparable. We shared so many similar values, enjoyed the outdoors together, and just seemed to click. Besides, he was handsome! Two years later, at the age of twenty-five, I married my first love, the one I had saved myself for. We had both kept ourselves pure—something that was very important to us, and as we shared our first kiss, it felt sacred and honorable before the Lord.

By this stage, I had purchased another property. I knew the investment 'rules', by now: 'Buy the worst house in the best street and do it up.' This house had a large, sub-dividable section and a house that was very run down, with blood-stains on the kitchen walls from the butchering that the previous owners used to carry out. Thick, treacle-like marks poured down the walls, and the linoleum around the toilet was saturated with urine. I remember dry wretching as I ran outside, lifting each revolting strip in my attempt to uncover the wooden floors three layers down. When we did reach the original floor it too was saturated with urine and was rotten through. Now we had to cut the rotten wood out and start afresh, but Jimmy and I were not afraid of hard work, and with a bit of elbow grease we managed to tidy it up.

The house was in an up-and-coming area, a good place to invest in, I thought, and although the property backed directly onto the motorway and had a large pylon running close by, I still had a good feeling about it. My dad, however, had a hard time coming to terms with what I could get for my money in the Auckland market, compared with what was available elsewhere.

By now I had begun working as a performing arts teacher, writing school productions, making short films, teaching fine arts across the school, leading the choir and putting on art exhibitions. My students were five to twelve year olds, and I was in heaven. I also had an incredible boss who gave me full creative license and let me do whatever I wanted. 'If you can imagine it, Cindy, then do it,' he would say to me. 'The more creative, the better.' It was an area of my life that I tapped into with a vengeance. The ideas flowed thick and fast; I felt alive and free in my innermost being.

VENTURING ABROAD

Jimmy and I had plans to travel to London before we began a family, but soon after we married, I fell pregnant with our first child, a beautiful, blue-eyed blondie who was the apple of my eye. We thought about our travel plans and decided we would just have to take him with us! My cousin was playing rugby in Ireland at the time and had mentioned that he may be able to get us work visas there. 'What a cool place to be,' we thought. 'So much more interesting than London, and far better to raise a child out of the city.'

By the time we had got organised, our baby son was one year old, and then, unexpectedly, I fell pregnant with our second child. 'Oh well,' I thought, 'they will both just have to come with us.' And so, we headed off to Galway, Ireland, a little seaside town on the west coast, famous for its performing arts, cobbled streets and colourful houses. I was six months pregnant, with our one year old, in tow. We went abroad with no job to go to, no home, no pregnancy care plan and just one suitcase each. I'm not sure if we were naive or just plain stupid! What I did know, was that we really had to rely on God to provide for all our needs. But for both Jimmy and myself, Ireland was our homeland, the land of our ancestors, and it felt very special to finally arrive.

We stayed with a couple who were good friends of my cousin while we looked for a place to rent, and Jimmy began applying for jobs. There was so much to pray for. In New Zealand, Jimmy had worked as a cameraman but had long held an interest in building; he had in fact just finished building the three bedroom home on the back of our section before we left. I had always thought that is where his passion lay, and so I encouraged him to apply for building jobs in Galway. Jimmy was prepared to do any sort of work to provide for his family. He even applied for a job cleaning the public toilets, and couldn't believe it when he was turned down for the job because he was considered overqualified. The employers were obviously concerned that he may not stick with the job if he found a better offer.

One day, I was reading the classifieds when I noticed an advertisement that read, 'Experienced carpenters need only apply.' Straight away I called the company and explained that Jimmy was a great builder but that he was terrible at promoting himself. Then I made them an offer. 'Look,' I said, 'He's better off showing you what he can do rather than telling you. Why doesn't he work a day for free, and if you like what you see, you can employ him. If you don't, then you have lost nothing either way.' 'Oh well then, when can he start?' they asked. 'Can he come down right now?' 'Well,' I replied, 'he's currently walking the streets approaching the building sites with his bag of hand tools, but as soon as he gets in, I'll send him down!'

Once he started, Jimmy never looked back. Whenever he was asked about his questionable (self-taught) methods he would simply reply, 'Oh, that's just how we do it in New Zealand.'

Just before Jimmy started work, we had agreed to lease a home in a lovely area called Knocknacarra, a fair way out on the outskirts of Galway. The trouble now was that Jimmy would need our car to get to work. I was concerned that I would be too isolated, living as a young mum out there on my own. But we had taken the house in faith, and so I shared my concerns with my cousin back in New Zealand, who prayed that I would be able to somehow use the car.

What an answer to prayer, then, when my husband accepted the job, only to hear the boss say, 'the only problem is that you will be working on a new subdivision which is a little bit further away. It's on the outskirts of town in a suburb called Knocknacarra. Would that be alright with you?' We couldn't believe it! Now Jimmy was able to walk to work; his build was in the very same block that we were moving into, and I was able to use the car for playgroups and midwife visits. God had gone before us, providing for our every need.

We moved into our two-storied house which was attached to a row of other houses. Every home looked exactly the same, except for the different coloured doorways. Our front door was a shiny forest green, and the place came fully furnished, with everything from lounge suites through to linen, cutlery and a television. There was even a Christmas tree up in the attic which we put to good use in December. We didn't have to provide for a single thing. Irish rental properties are usually rented out with basic furniture, but the other household items are not usually included. Our owner, however, had decided that he wanted to travel and didn't want to bother with shifting any of his things out.

There were so many answered prayers along the way as we began to settle in. At one stage I needed a baby rocker so that I could feed our toddler and keep the newborn baby happy at the same time. The next day there was a knock at the door, and there, sitting on the doorstep, was a baby rocker but no-one in sight. I couldn't believe it. 'Lord, that was just a thought! I hadn't even asked for it, but before I had the chance to ask, you had already provided for us.'

I found that God provided for us in very specific ways. I had been feeling anxious about our eldest son's development, and with the new baby coming, I had also begun to worry. How would I know if my children were developing at the right stages? Unsure of the usual markers, and what to expect, I asked God to help me. Within the week, a lovely women from the new church we had begun to attend, came and handed me a book on child development from birth to two year old's! She did not know what I had prayed for but felt prompted to offer it to me.

During our time in Ireland, God showed me that he was able to provide for our every need, that when we put our trust in him, he delights in it. Looking back, that time became a benchmark for me, a season where my faith grew, as I learned to completely trust in him for all our needs. The Lord also showed me that he was very concerned not only with my needs, but with the desires of my heart. A short three months after we had settled in Ireland, it was time for our baby to arrive. My parents had planned to come over during that time, taking a punt with dates in the hope that they would have a week to spend with us before the birth and then a week with us afterwards. The only problem was that our firstborn had arrived ten days before his due date, and so we really didn't know when to expect our second child's arrival.

By now, my parents had been with us a week already. 'What if the baby doesn't come while they are here?' I began to worry. And so I prayed, 'Lord you know I really would like mum and dad to see their grandchild, and they are halfway through their visit already. God, if you could please bring me into labour to-morrow, I'd be really grateful. I'd also love a good night's sleep, so if I could go into labour in the morning, that would be awe-some! Oh, and if I could have breakfast first too, that would be really great. Thanks God.'

What must he think when we pray these prayers?! I think he loves it, just like an earthly father loves the innocent requests of his own children.

The next day I sat down to have my favourite breakfast, a piece of toast and a boiled egg. As I placed the very last mouthful of egg in my mouth, yes—my first contraction began! 'What an incredibly loving father you are to me,' I thought. Then the chaos began. As soon as I went into labour, the contractions came thick and fast. Jimmy was just leaving to fill the car up with gas when I yelled out, 'Mum! Tell him to come back. We have no time, the baby is coming right now!'

We drove down the extremely rickety roads on an empty tank, with me feeling every painful bump. Arriving at the hospital, we passed through the front doors, took a left turn and saw ahead of us an enormously long corridor to the maternity ward. I could not believe it. 'Only in Ireland,' I thought to myself. I barely made it to the delivery room. We had only minutes to spare, but after just one and a half hours of labour, our beautiful daughter was born. With her head of thick black hair, here was our little Irish lass, and now we were able to enjoy a very special week with my parents and their new grandchild. 'God had it all covered, didn't he?' I thought. 'What was all that worry about?'

A NEW JOURNEY BEGINS

A year passed, and by that time, our working visa was about to expire. It was time to move on. We had saved hard while we were in Ireland, getting a boarder in to make extra money, and had managed to pull together enough funds to buy a campervan. Our plan was to travel around Europe for three months before we headed back home to New Zealand. Our daughter was nine months old, and I wanted to be home in time for her first birthday. We had saved exactly two thousand Euro, which had been our goal. We had made it! It really wasn't much to buy a campervan, we knew that, but we weren't fussy—we just wanted anything that would get us from A to B.

I had heard that in London there was a car fair where it was possible to buy cheap campervans, so I sent Jimmy over to London to pick one up and drive it back to Galway. He had a weekend to do it in, no pressure! Still, he was a bit freaked out by the thought of picking the wrong one. 'Oh, you'll be fine,' I said and waved him off.

Jimmy arrived at the car fair only to find that there was not one campervan or car on site! But we had no plan B; he had to find a campervan that weekend and bring it back—after all, he had to be back at work on Monday in Ireland. Scrambling around, Jimmy managed to find one elsewhere and soon after, began the trip home. It was only minutes later that I received a call from Jimmy's sister in London. 'Oh Cindy,' she said, 'I've just said goodbye to Jimmy and given instructions on where to go, but I'm looking out the window and at the very first turn he has gone left and not right. He has no map, and I don't know how he's going to get out of London and make it to the ferry on time!'

I will never forget the day he arrived back. Our baby daughter was in the stroller and I was walking with her big brother. We were coming back from the corner store when I heard a horn beeping over and over. When I turned around, I put my hand over my mouth and gasped! Jimmy was driving the most hilarious looking campervan I had ever seen! We laughed and laughed. What in the world were we doing?

Shortly afterwards we headed off with our two little ones in tow. This time, we had a plan. We were going to head up into Northern Ireland, then catch the ferry down to France. From there we would travel through Spain, then back across southern France and into Italy and Greece, before making our way back through Switzerland and then back to England and home within three months.

We decided we would spend most of our time meandering around the quaint villages, and only spend a day or so in the major cities. And so, we parked the camper on the outskirts, then biked into the cities for the day. It was a perfect arrangement, with our little boy perched in a toddler seat behind Jimmy, and the baby in a backpack with me. In the end, having two little ones in tow wasn't so bad after all, and ours were at the perfect age. Our son was not so old that he wanted to walk everywhere, and our wee daughter sat snugly in my backpack as we roamed around.

We were mesmerised with France and quickly fell in love with its charm. The wine was inexpensive, only two Euro for a bottle at the time, and with local cheeses, meats and pastries on offer, we slowed right down, enjoyed the small villages and took a lot longer than we had anticipated. Eventually we continued on our way, dipping into Spain and then heading back out to the south of France. We were heading for Italy, through idyllic, picturesque little villages.

STICKS AND STONES

Eventually we came to a small town close to the Italian border. It was bustling with tourists, and we joined in, swimming at the beach and walking up the hill to a historic site that looked out over charming terracotta rooftops and beyond, to the sea. We had been 'free-camping' along the way, trying, if possible, to park alongside other campervans nearby, which felt, not only more sociable, but safer as well. That day, the campers were mostly parked on the road that ran along the beachfront, rather than on the busier main road slightly higher up which led to the Italian border.

We settled in for the night as usual, amongst the convoy of other campers, until suddenly, somewhere around eleven p.m. we were woken by an almighty THUD—and then another! The noise startled Jimmy, who jumped up and waited in silence. Then it came again. THUD! Someone, it seemed, was throwing rocks at our campervan! 'Yes,' I thought, 'we are an easy target, *the oldest craziest-looking campervan of the lot.*'

Jimmy peered out the window and waited until there were no more hits. He wanted to see who had thrown the rocks but could see no one. Not being one to back down, however, he opened the door to inspect the damage and have a look around. He was going to confront whoever it was that had done this. Meanwhile, I was feeling nervous. My heart was racing, and I felt suddenly very vulnerable being left on my own with the children as I watched my husband disappear out of sight.

Jimmy walked up to the main road to see if there was any sign of trouble, but found nothing. As he turned to come back to the camper, however, a mob of guys emerged from the darkness, each of them wielding wooden battens as thick as my arm—and twice as long. Bored and drunk, they were on the lookout to make trouble with the tourists. Not just a week earlier, we had heard, someone travelling through the region had been shot dead. It was only the beginning of the tourist season, yet restlessness was brewing amongst some of the local thugs.

Jimmy quickened his pace as he began walking back towards the van, trying to ignore them as they called out in French. But the mob were closing in on him, and he could sense what was about to come. With no further warning, the men set on him, taking swings at him and hitting him around the head, blow after blow, with full force. The mob was determined to get Jimmy onto the ground; kicking and whacking him over and over again, they continued to lay into him, until Jimmy got a burst of adrenaline. Picking up one of the men, he lifted him high up above his head as if he were a feather weight, and turned towards a nearby pizza restaurant with a metal fence beside it. 'I could either impale him on this fence and kill him right now or I can throw him through the shop window to scare the others off,' Jimmy thought, but already he had made his choice. He would spare the drunk man's life. Seeing their mate held above Jimmy's head, however, was enough to send the others off scattering like cockroaches into the old walled city. Placing the man down, Jimmy slumped against the concrete railing. He had just been attacked by a gang of ten to one and survived.

By the time the police arrived, they had been able to catch just a few of the men, while the rest seemed to have got away. At the exact same time in New Zealand, we later discovered, a family friend had felt prompted to pray for Jimmy. As a result, Jimmy had felt nothing while he was being attacked. He also had managed to stay on his feet—though now he was sure that if the mob had been able to get him to the ground, he would have certainly died.

Back in the campervan, I could hear the disturbance coming from the top road and had gone outside to see what was happening. Not wanting to leave my children alone, I ran to the campervan that was parked behind ours. Inside were a lovely Welsh couple who were travelling with their three-year-old daughter. We had met them that day on the beach; now, I asked if the man would come with me up to the main road to see if Jimmy was alright, because I knew he was in trouble. Kindly, his wife stood guard between the two campers watching our children as they slept on, peacefully unaware of the commotion.

When we reached the top road, I found Jimmy with blood streaming down his face and badly shaken. Fuming, I began to yell at the police in broken French, telling them that 'this was not okay, it was totally unacceptable, and *what were they going to do about it?*' Their response was that they had officers out looking for the other offenders, but that it was going to be very difficult to find them in the maze of the old city streets. 'In the meantime,' they said, 'we will take Jimmy to the hospital to get him stitched up and then we will bring him back to you.' They also told me that it was not safe for me to remain parked where I was, since the remaining gang members might return later on to attack me when I was on my own.

The police decided to set up a guard around the campervan until I found the keys, then they would escort me out of France, where I could wait in a carpark across the Italian border until Jimmy was discharged from hospital and could be returned to me. I was in shock. I had never driven the campervan before, I had no idea where the keys were, and it felt very much like the police were washing their hands of this whole this mess by moving us on as quickly as possible into another country!

I searched everywhere in the campervan for the car keys while the police stood guard outside until, half an hour later, I found them. Jimmy had placed the keys behind the felt lining of the campervan wall, next to the driver's seat, and how I even managed to locate them, I do not know. As I pulled away and drove down the road with police in a great convoy of motorbikes, flashing their lights in front and behind me, it felt very surreal, and a stream of thoughts raced through my mind. *What in the world is happening right now? Can I even drive this beast of a thing? Where is Jimmy? Is he okay? Where are you taking me?*

The police pulled up in a dark, empty car park and left me there, where I sat numbly on the bed for hours and hours. At four a.m. there was a rap on the door, and there was Jimmy. The police had brought him back to me and now they simply drove off, leaving us there. We held each other tightly, curled up like a fetus together on the bed, and began to weep. Trauma had visited us on that very dark night.

FEELING NUMB

The next day the Welsh couple came looking for us. They had just travelled through Italy and were heading in the opposite direction to us, but when they found us, they offered to take us to a small Italian village nearby to recover for a few days. It was our son's birthday that day. He was three years old. Time to celebrate. It is intriguing to me, that even in a numb state of shock, you can almost do anything, that you can somehow carry on as if life is normal. What we didn't know at the time, was that life for us would never be normal again.

That day, we strung up party streamers, attempted to buy icing sugar for the cake while speaking no Italian whatsoever, and had to return to the store three times with flour or whatever other white substance we had purchased that was not what we needed! I bought cupcakes and placed them together to resemble a caterpillar, decorated them with some green-coloured icing after we finally found the right ingredients, put smarties all over the caterpillar and even dismantled a cupboard door from the campervan and covered it with tinfoil to create a base for the cake to sit on. We sang happy birthday, blew party whistles, let off party poppers, rang nana and granddad in New Zealand who wished their grandson a happy birthday, and even managed to go on a birthday treasure hunt with our new-found friends.

Though everything appeared the same as ever, nothing could have been further from reality; everything was, in fact, *abnormal* . . . and surreal. All I knew was that we needed a place to catch our breath—and so we decided to head to the home of a loyal and caring friend who had been a bridesmaid at our wedding and now lived in a little town in the French Alps, about two hour's drive from where we were. There, we could rest and stay while we recovered from the ordeal of the previous night.

BREATHING SPACE

My friend was engaged to a French man whose family lived nearby. It was his sister, a nurse, who first expressed concern. 'You need to get your head checked out at the local hospital,' she said to Jimmy when she heard that he had spent most of the first few days simply sitting in the corner of the loungeroom, staring into midair. But Jimmy refused. He just wanted to go home, he said. Jimmy's dad, on hearing the news, offered to fly over immediately and bring us all back home. 'Don't worry about the details,' he said. 'You can even ditch the camper on the side of the road. Just come home . . .' The love of his father was touching.

It was clear, after that week, that we would not be able to continue with our trip, and so we decided to make a beeline back to London where we would try to sell the campervan and arrange our flights home. After making a few calls, it turned out that my brother's friends, who lived in London, were about to go away on holiday for two weeks. Those two weeks, it just so happened, were when we would be needing somewhere to stay—and, to top it off, their home was right beside Heathrow Airport. So we set off, straight back up to London, where for the next week, we rested, tried to recover a little, and managed to sell the campervan. Then, when everything had fallen into place, we boarded a plane back home with our tails between our legs.

What occurred in France would change the course of our lives forever. We were not to fully understand why, or what had happened, until many, many years later, when it all came out in the wash . . .

PART 2

returning

When we arrived back home, we decided to rent a house in a more rural area. We wanted to see if country living might suit us as a long-term plan, but while the peace and tranquility was lovely, we found ourselves hankering to be closer to the city. And so we began looking for a place to buy on the fringes of West Auckland.

One of the issues was that as soon as we arrived back to New Zealand, Jimmy's behaviour became erratic. Suddenly, he began to have angry outbursts, being short with the children and terribly irritable. It was as if he were having a personality change right in front of me. I was worried that something had happened internally as a result of the knocks he had taken to the head, and asked him to go to the doctors with me. I even arranged a babysitter and booked the appointment, but he flatly refused to go.

Eventually, I laid it to rest; we just got on with life as best we could. Things were not great, but neither were they completely terrible. Over time, I put Jimmy's behaviour down to his temperament, his personality. I figured he just wasn't into kids, didn't enjoy celebrations and simply wasn't a 'family man,' and resigned myself to the fact that this was just who he was. As the years went by, however, things got progressively worse. Toys got smashed, the kids were being yelled at, and we began to feel as if we were walking around on eggshells in our own home.

Soon we began looking for properties to purchase and were thankful when my dad found us a 'deal.' This house was part of a subdivision, and would give us a place to live while we developed the land around it into property lots. We felt a little out of our depth taking on a project of that size, but it looked promising and we decided to give it a go. Then, just as we were about to sign the agreement, my dad said to the owners, 'I just want to hold off signing for one more day. I'd like to get a second opinion from my land surveyor and then I'll come back to you tomorrow.' The owners agreed and we said goodbye.

My dad knew a land surveyor that he had used for many years and called on him for a second opinion. 'What's the address of the property you are looking at?' he asked. When we told him, he stood up, asked us to wait a moment, and left the room. Minutes later, he returned, placing a massive file down on the desk. 'Because I know you so well,' he said, 'and because of our long-standing relationship, I am going to show you something which I probably shouldn't. I can hardly believe this is happening. As you know, I have just moved up to Auckland and this is the first job I have completed for a client here. I am not supposed to show you this because he has paid for it and it is officially his private document, but he engaged me to survey the exact piece of land you are looking at purchasing.' Then he said, 'I'll tell you what you should do with that property—you should run a mile. That whole piece of land is completely unstable and is slipping. You will never be able to subdivide that land and you will lose a lot of money over it.'

I couldn't believe it. What were the chances that in all of Auckland, and of all the properties this surveyor from central Auckland could have worked on, his first job would have been on the very piece of land that we were looking at purchasing! 'That was certainly no coincidence,' I thought. It was also no coincidence that my dad had felt prompted to stall the deal proceedings and that now we were being handed a lifeline. 'I'm really sorry to be the bearer of bad news,' the surveyor said, to which my dad replied, 'Don't be sorry! You have just saved us a lot of money. We are going to go and celebrate!'

The Lord had firmly shut that door behind us and in so doing, spared us an awful lot of trouble and loss. I felt so safe knowing that God had our backs. 'When you walk through the fire, you will not be burned,' I recalled. 'Yes,' I thought, 'God is walking beside us, and is for us, because he loves us.'

We came away from that experience knowing what we *didn't* want, that's for sure! We didn't want to take on a big project like that. We just wanted a family home somewhere rural but close enough to the city and still 'out West.' Soon, we settled on an area we liked and began to write out our wish list. It needed to be within our budget—we were firm on that. One hundred and seventy thousand dollars was our limit. We also wanted a four-bedroom home with a bath and a fireplace, and with that, we simply prayed and committed our requests to the Lord.

The very next day, we got a call from an old friend who lived in that area. 'Hey, I hear you might be looking buy a place out our way. I was just talking to my neighbour over the fence yesterday who mentioned that they are going to be putting their house on the market. It's a four-bedroom split level place.' 'How much do they want for it, do you know?' Jimmy asked. 'They're looking at one hundred and ninety thousand,' he replied, 'but if they can sell it privately they would take one hundred and seventy.' I couldn't believe it. Just as quickly as God had shut one door, he was opening another!

We bought the place and settled in to our first family home, complete with bath and fireplace, in a small rural community only ten minutes from the beach, the local mall and the city motorway. It was a fantastic place to raise our kids and we loved it there! Soon, our third child was born, bringing us all great joy. All our children went to the local kindergarten and primary school, and as a family, we became entrenched in the life of the community. I was a stay-at-home mum until my children reached school age; then, when our youngest son turned five, I began teaching art again, just three days a week.

Jimmy was working as a local builder, and we tried our best to lead happy, normal lives. I had inherited my father's positivity and always strived to make the best out of any situation, but underneath it all, there was a dark and swift undercurrent. Jimmy's outbursts were becoming increasingly erratic and confronting. I spent many days on the couch, crying in private as I grieved over the way my children were being treated. 'How can he treat them this way?' I thought. 'He is their father!' One thing I knew for certain, things were not normal, they were not okay, and the whole situation was certainly getting worse.

SOULMATES

During this time, I became very close friends with a woman called Michelle who was wonderful in every way. I gravitated towards her zest for life, her passion for her community, and her love for people. We were polar opposites to look at—I was a tall, young, six-foot-two blonde white woman, and Michelle was a short Maori woman in her thirties with jet black hair. But we clicked, forming a deep love for one another. Michelle was like a soul mate to me; I had always sought out mentors in my life and was attracted to spiritual qualities in other women that I longed to nurture within myself. But she was more than that to me. We simply understood one another. Michelle imparted so much of her influence into my life.

It was only a few years later, driving home from a doctor's appointment with her husband, when she called me from the car.

'Are you sitting down?' she asked. I held my breath, knowing something was wrong. 'I've just been diagnosed with breast cancer,' she said. I was devastated. Michelle passed away and I grieved hard. I missed her terribly—and still do. Some days, I long to see her again, to sit and chat together, to ask her advice, to pray together, and when things get difficult, I have a deep yearning to be near her again.

ANGELS

When I look back over their childhood, I realise that God has indeed been very close to my children and walked beside them every step of the way. Every time we hit the difficult low points, I would cry out to God and ask him to reveal himself to my kids, to show them that he was real. I not only wanted them to know him with their minds, but in their hearts. I wanted them to see feel and experience his presence with them. I prayed that God would give each and every one of them a spiritual encounter with him . . . and in response, God sent his angels.

My eldest son was being confronted from every direction; it was hard at home and equally challenging at school. He was just nine years old the day his friends deserted him, and he recalls feeling very lonely. As he walked through a wind tunnel that connected two classrooms, he suddenly felt compelled to turn around, and there, in front of him, stood a mighty angel! It was massive—at least ten feet tall; it went right through the roof as it stood there. The encounter was fleeting, and just as quickly as it had appeared, the angel vanished. I told my son that we have guardian angels that watch over us and care for us, and reassured him that we are never alone. 'For he will command his angels concerning you to guard you in all your ways[1].'

---

1   Psalm 91:11

My daughter was only six years old when one day, she saw a bright light rushing through the house. She chased it up the stairs as it ran into the kitchen and passed right through the closed pantry doors. She too, had seen an angel, and I am sure she kept that treasured moment hidden in her heart.

A RECIPE FOR DISASTER

We lived in that township for eight years before selling up and buying a piece of land to build on. It was always a dream of ours to do this together, and so, while we began building, we moved our young family into a converted garage that belonged to some friends and was sitting empty. The garage was very tight—it had one open space with a tiny bathroom in it, and we partitioned off a bedroom in one corner, just enough space to fit our double bed in and a handmade three-storied bunkbed that Jimmy had built. It was so tiny that the kids had to slip into their beds like little envelopes, and our eldest son, who slept on the top bunk, could not sit up in bed without hitting his head on the roof! I could lean over from our bed and touch the children's bunk, it was that close.

Jimmy was pragmatic. 'We'll only be here for a three to six months,' he reassured me. 'By that time, I'll have things processed through council, build the barn, and before you know it, we'll be moved in!' How naive we were—but it sounded good to me, and we all agreed that we could do it. And so we all ended up living on top of one another, which, for any normal family, would have been extremely challenging, but with our family dynamics, was a complete recipe for disaster.

By now, I was tiptoeing around the place, trying to keep the peace at home, always looking for ways to avoid Jimmy's angry outbursts, and trying to read his behaviour—learning what provoked him, what agitated him, what made him annoyed, and how we might avoid triggering him at all costs. It required an incredible amount of mental energy; living on high alert day after day became so very draining. It seemed that no matter what I did, it was never good enough, there would always be another angry outburst at home.

DECLINING HEALTH

Gradually, my health had been declining. Over the past couple of years, I had become depressed and anxious, and I was not in a good way. I was desperate to get help for Jimmy, knowing deep down in my spirit that something was wrong with him—I just didn't know what it was. When he complained that he was getting tension headaches between his eyes, I badgered him to go to the doctor to get them checked out, and as a result, Jimmy was referred to a sinus specialist, which made him feel that we were making progress. After many tests, however, the specialist came back to us and told us there were definitely no sinus issues. 'You do have a grossly disfigured nose, though!' he said. 'What?!' I thought. 'Firstly, his nose looks just fine to me, and secondly, if he doesn't have sinus issues, then what the heck is going on with him?' We had hit a brick wall, it seemed, and it left us feeling despondent, somewhat frustrated, and altogether strung out. Not knowing what to do next, we simply laid it to rest for a bit longer.

BREATHLESS

Jimmy was born with an A-typical personality, very black and white, strong willed and stubborn—which had its positives and negatives, depending which way you chose to look at it. During our time at the garage he developed a cough, for example, which he ignored for four months, refusing to see a doctor. Eventually, the cough travelled right down to his chest, until one afternoon he went out for a walk and came home wheezing and puffing so hard he could barely make it back up the hill. By now his cough sounded like nothing I had ever heard, and I was scared. With a strong quickening in my spirit, I yelled at him, which I would never normally have done. 'You have got to go to the doctor! You are seriously unwell!' But he didn't go; he simply went to bed as usual.

I will never forget what happened when I awoke the following morning. Jimmy was sitting, buckled over on the side of the bed, rasping, 'Cindy! I can't breathe, I can't breathe. Take me to the hospital!' My blood froze. I knew instantly that this was serious, so I picked up the kids, threw everyone in the car, and made a beeline down the driveway to our friend's place. 'Please, quick! Take the kids!' I yelled as I dragged the children from the back seat. 'Jimmy can't breathe!'

There was no time to say anything else, and with the kids still standing there looking stunned, I took off at full speed, racing to the hospital until we arrived at the Accident & Emergency entrance. 'It's just asthmatic symptoms,' the staff decided when they had brought Jimmy into the examination room. 'We'll just put him on the nebuliser.' For nearly an hour, Jimmy breathed through the nebuliser mask, but even the staff could see that his breath was still heavily laboured and he was not improving. 'We need to get you to a main hospital as soon as possible,' they soon agreed, and quickly arranged for Jimmy to be transferred by ambulance.

The medical team at the city hospital took tests and tried to re-assure us that Jimmy was doing well, however, his breathing was getting more difficult and things were looking grim. By now, it was nearly ten a.m. and Jimmy had been battling for three long hours, gasping for each and every breath. Sure enough, the test results showed that the carbon dioxide levels in Jimmy's blood were rising dangerously. The hospital staff began speaking to me, but I could not understand the terms they were using. All I could gather was that they were going to perform a medical procedure to help him breathe more easily. I felt incredibly relieved. 'Yes, yes,' I said, 'do whatever you need to help him breathe better.' I was beside myself, but I had to sign some forms . . . and then a medic looked at me, and in the most compassionate way put his arm on my shoulder, and said gently and quietly, 'Maybe you should go and say a few final words before we get the procedure started.' I looked at him strangely and felt an immense sense of uneasiness creep over me. 'What the heck is going on here?' I thought. 'What are you telling me? I don't understand what you are saying.'

At that point, one of the nurses realised that I wasn't aware of what they were about to do. Taking me aside, she said, 'Do you understand what we are saying here?' 'No,' I replied, 'what exactly are you saying?' By now, I was nervous. 'We are going to induce your husband into a coma,' she explained. I was in shock. *What?! A coma!?* I could not believe that it had got so serious, so quickly. 'We are bringing a specialist team over from the North Shore Hospital,' she said. 'They are on their way with the life support machine.' Quickly, I rang my father-in-law, who arrived in record time to find Jimmy barely able to breathe.

The specialist team arrived, and I will never forget them standing in a large semi-circle around Jimmy's bed, waiting to be given the green light to begin inducing the coma. 'Just give her a moment please,' one of them said, and they all stepped back to give me some space. I walked over to Jimmy in a daze. What do you say when you are face to face with your husband and you think it may be the last time that you will ever see him again? And what do you say with an audience there? I bent down and spoke gently into his ear. 'You are going to be okay, Jimmy. They are going to give you something to help you breathe. I love you and I'll see you soon.'

With that, I walked out of the room, walked around the corner of the corridor, collapsed on the floor and wept. I was overcome with grief. Jimmy's dad was talking on his phone when suddenly I heard an almighty commotion coming from the resuscitation room. Getting up, I ran to see what was going on. The alarms were going the curtain was closed around Jimmy's bed, but I could see Jimmy flailing about on the ground, and there was blood everywhere. 'Security, security! Somebody, quick, we need security here now!' they were calling.

Jimmy, feeling himself fall into a coma, had pulled every cord and tube out of his body as he gasped for his last breath of air in an almighty surge to fight for his life. Every vital line that was keeping him alive was now strewn around the room. Within seconds, security arrived, rushing in and pinning him down to the ground. They had no time to place him back on the bed—Jimmy was turning blue, he had stopped breathing and was losing oxygen to his brain. Quickly, the resuscitation team shoved the tubes back down Jimmy's neck and turned on the machines that would now breathe for him. *The fragility of life.*

Once Jimmy was stabilised, the life support machine activated, and the room cleaned up, a nurse pulled back the curtain and asked if I would like to come in and see him. Seeing Jimmy lying there so peacefully, I felt so relieved that he was no longer fighting for his breath. I stroked his forehead and kissed him on the cheek. It was so bizarre, knowing that he was in a coma, yet feeling so grateful for the machine that was doing all the work for him; the fact that he no longer had to gasp for air, in some way, brought me great comfort and peace.

Jimmy was then transferred to another hospital by ambulance, where he was taken straight to the intensive care unit and placed in an isolation room where he could be monitored around the clock. He was critically ill. Soon, all of the specialists in the unit called a meeting. We sat around a boardroom table—Jimmy's parents, my parents and myself, along with the intensive care team, who began to describe to us what was going on.

'He has a raging infection,' one doctor explained. 'We can't contain it and we don't know what it is. It's travelled down into his lungs and seems to be shutting them down. We believe he has a twenty per cent chance of survival if he makes it through the first night. If he does make it through tonight, then we predict that he will remain in a coma for six weeks and will need to be in hospital for a minimum of three months to rehabilitate.' The statistics were out, and it was pretty grim news to absorb. 'In the meantime,' they said, 'we are going to put a whole pile of antibiotics into his system and hope that we can beat the infection before it takes over his body.'

A MIRACLE

Jimmy went into the coma at ten a.m. that day—and he made it through that night. The pastor of our local church arrived at the hospital when he heard the news, and I was incredibly grateful for our loving and supportive church family. He sat with me as I told him about Jimmy's chances of survival, and how he would be in a coma for six weeks and in hospital for three months thereafter to recover. Looking at me, our pastor responded, 'Well, I can't see those time frames working out too well for your family.' I was a little taken aback at the strangely humorous comment. 'As if you can do anything about that!' I thought to myself. 'Shall we pray?' he then offered, and sitting together, in the waiting room he prayed a very simple prayer, asking the Lord to heal Jimmy and grant him a quick recovery. 'Can I go in and see Jimmy?' my pastor asked, and so I led him through to the little room where the nurse was watching my husband and fiddling constantly with dials to correct his oxygen levels.

As we walked into the room, I noticed a slightly bewildered expression come over the face of Jimmy's nurse. 'Oh, that's strange,' she said, looking up at me. 'What's going on?' I asked. Looking back at Jimmy once again, she fiddled around a bit more and then said, 'He just started to breathe on his own!' It was as if the Lord had almost instantly answered our prayers. I looked at the clock. *Ten a.m.* Exactly twenty-four hours after Jimmy had gone into the coma, he had begun to breathe on his own—and then, seven days later, to the very hour, he was discharged from hospital. At ten a.m. that incredible day, we walked back out through the hospital doors! The medics were stunned. Such a rapid recovery went against all the odds. It was an absolute miracle.

NEW INSIGHTS

Sadly, the story did not end there, though I wish it might have. If I had thought things couldn't get worse, I was wrong. Having made it through this latest trauma, we were now in a state of euphoria. Wanting to celebrate that Jimmy was alive and well, we took off to the South Island for three weeks in a campervan, meandering through the stunning scenery, taking in the sights and enjoying our family with fresh eyes and a newfound appreciation for life itself. We were together and that was all that really mattered.

The moment we returned to our tiny garage-home, however, Jimmy's symptoms returned with a vengeance. My anxiety came flooding back too as I tried to manage his agitation, angry outbursts and verbal lashings. My husband had an unusually short wick, even for him, and suddenly I felt like I was drowning. What was going on?

One day as we sat around the dining room table, I looked over at my son and noticed that his hand was shaking badly as he tried to carefully place his spoon in his mouth. He was staring at his dad wide-eyed, trying so hard not to clink the spoon against the side of his mouth in case he got yelled at for making a noise. That was the moment that broke me inside.

We had all been living in fear, I now realised, and knowing that this was no way to live, I booked in to see a counsellor. I was no longer coping—the counsellor could see that—and if I continued to live like this, she said, I would have a complete breakdown. 'It's not a matter of 'if' but 'when',' she said, and recommended that I take some time out from my situation and give Jimmy an ultimatum. Either he sought out professional help, or I would need to move on without him.

This sort of thinking went against every fibre of my being. I had been raised with a high regard for marriage, and taught that a woman should never leave her husband. But things had gotten out of hand. By this time, I was very unwell; besides, I had a responsibility to take care of my children, and so far, Jimmy had simply been unwilling to get help. 'How long do you recommend I leave for?' I asked the counsellor, thinking she would say a couple of weeks. 'Three to six months,' she replied. I was shocked. As I drove home from the appointment, my mind was reeling as I tried to take it all in.

'Okay,' Lord, I prayed. 'If you are truly in this, then you are going to have make it abundantly clear to me that this is the right thing to do. I will move out for three to six months, but where will I go? What landlord in their right mind would want me for such a short time? I'm not going to lie to a landlord and say that I will take a property for a year, which is the usual minimum requirement,' I insisted. 'I'll have to be honest and tell them I only want it short-term, so how are you going to find me a place like that?'

I drove back to the garage and sat down in front of the computer. My hand began to tremble as I placed it over the mouse. *What in the world am I doing?* I thought to myself. *This is totally insane.* I decided to look at houses close to where we now lived and was utterly surprised when the very first house that popped up on my screen said, 'Short-term rental—three to six months only.' I was stunned! The Lord certainly had my attention, but I could not understand what was going on—this defied all my logic, all my 'Christian beliefs' about what was the right thing to do, and yet the Lord seemed to be giving an undeniable directive. I just had to trust that he knew what he was doing.

Within the week, things were all set, and my parents had offered to come to help me move. I had given him the ultimatum, 'Get help or else it's over between us,' but Jimmy was reeling from the news and couldn't believe what was happening. Nor could I, truth be told. That Friday night, I was supposed to be at an event I had organised as the leader of the women's ministry at our church. *What an absolute hypocrite,* I thought to myself. *You are running a ministry and yet here you are about to leave your marriage.*

I was moving out the very next morning but decided to go to the event anyway. After all, I was in charge. Normally those of us on the team would meet in the prayer room half an hour before the event started, but on that particular night, only one other woman showed up to pray. That was unusual, but we sat down, and she asked me how Jimmy was getting on. I presumed she was talking about his recovery from the coma. 'He's not great, actually,' I responded. 'Oh,' she replied, 'mine's not either,' and she began to describe a long list of symptoms . . . the very same symptoms Jimmy also had. 'It sounds like you are describing Jimmy,' I said. Looking me squarely in the face, she said, 'Well, if you have never heard the term before, I am telling you, your husband has a Traumatic Brain Injury.'

What? I could not believe it. I had never even heard of the term before, but now it made sense: short wick, angry outbursts, irritability, headaches between the eyes, sensitivity to noise, light and movement, poor sleep . . . the list went on. God had shown up that night in his grace and mercy, showing me at the eleventh hour just what we were dealing with. I couldn't get Jimmy to go to a doctor, so he sent someone to me to deliver the prognosis instead. It was no coincidence that there was just one woman at the prayer meeting that night when normally there would be five of us.

When the event had ended, I rang Jimmy immediately. I felt so excited. God had given us a key. Now we knew what we were dealing with. I knew I still needed time out to recover, but I explained to him that I felt he was to go to the doctors and ask to be checked out for a possible Traumatic Head Injury. 'I'll come with you,' I said.

The following week, I moved with the kids into a spacious, sun-filled home, and felt the relief instantly. This was a place of rest, peace and calm, a place where the Lord began reminding me of some powerful scriptures.

'The Lord is my shepherd; I shall not want.
He makes me lie down in green pastures.
He leads me beside still waters.
He restores my soul . . .
Even though I walk through the valley of the shadow of death,
I will fear no evil, for you are with me;
Your rod and your staff,
They comfort me . . .
Surely goodness and mercy shall follow me
all the days of my life,
and I shall dwell in the house of the Lord forever.[2]

Around the same time, a church member called me out of the blue; he barely knew me, but he said, 'I believe the Lord has given me a scripture for you. It's Psalm twenty-three.' Once again, I had confirmation that the Lord was by my side.

Despite my hopefulness, Jimmy still refused to go to the doctor. In the meantime, friends offered for him to stay with them, but instead he chose to live in some old, leaking, rusty containers that had been plonked on our land. These were very dark days for him—it was cold, damp and very wet in the middle of winter. He

---

2   Psalm 23

set up a pup tent in the middle of the container, with rats scurrying all around, but he didn't mind. All he wanted was peace and quiet, and instinctively he knew that's what his brain needed.

SEPARATION

The nights were the hardest for me during our time of separation. I would curl up and weep like a baby throughout the night, feeling absolutely tormented. Terrible lies filled my mind; Satan was having a real go at me, but I found that as quickly as a negative thought would come, a verse would also come to combat that thought. It was like a boxing match that went on and on in my mind, but all night long, the Lord would reveal truths to me. There were nights where I could barely sleep, it was such a 'battle of the mind,' but I began speaking scriptures out loud, claiming every word, every declaration and promise. It was the only way I found peace in my life during that time. The Lord just flooded my mind with scripture.

I was so grateful that as a child my faith had been firmly built on biblical truths and memory verses. That ammunition may have been sitting dormant, but it was ready just when I needed it. Every time I felt despondent, scriptures came to my mind . . . they were there almost instantly, exactly the words I needed to negate the lies. Day and night, I would speak scriptural truths out loud, typing or writing them out and claiming them. I went around the house speaking in tongues, then would pause to write out the truths that the Lord had been revealing to me. Soon, notes were everywhere . . . above the vanity in the bathroom, beside the kitchen bench, even in my car! And then, I put worship music on, flooding my life with truth and allowing the presence of the Holy Spirit to permeate my whole being.

I began to carry an incredible peace during my time of separation from Jimmy, knowing that the Lord was in it and that he was directing my paths. 'The steps of a good man (or woman) are ordered by the Lord.'[3] As upside down as my life seemed at the time, I had totally put my trust my hope and confidence in the Lord, and was at peace.

Finally, Jimmy came and told me that he was going to see the doctor. That was a turning point for us. We asked the doctor for a referral to a neuropsychologist so that Jimmy could be tested thoroughly. The full test lasted for five hours—with puzzles and quizzes and other means of seeing how each section of Jimmy's brain was activated, and then comparing the results with standardised norms. It didn't take long for the doctor to come to the conclusion: 'Jimmy, you have a severe traumatic brain injury.' All it took, then, was for a report to be put together and suddenly, there it was, in black and white. Finally we had a diagnosis, something we could work with. 'The biggest problem with head injury patients,' he said, 'is denial. Often the patients do not actually believe they have a head injury.'

Very slowly, Jimmy came to terms with the fact that he did, in fact, have a brain injury and that we needed to do something about it. Soon, home visits commenced, with a specialist from the head injury clinic working alongside us as a family. Together we came up with strategies that could help us live together more harmoniously, prevent Jimmy from causing any more damage to us as a family, and enable us to avoid causing further trauma to Jimmy as well. We learned how both of us could have our needs met, and how to work better together. With meetings in place to track how we were going, Jimmy slowly improved, and we were

---

3   Psalm 27:3

able to put the pieces back together to the point where he moved back in with us.

Because the attack had happened in France, and so long ago, Jimmy was not eligible for any accident compensation—we just did not fit the criteria for financial assistance. That effectively meant that that I was thrust back into work, despite being heavily medicated for depression at the time. Tanked up on pills, I went back to teaching fulltime for six weeks, and somehow we managed to get through that period, even though I had to sit in a chair to teach because I was so weak and often had the shakes.

It was during that time that a lovely woman from our church who barely knew us, started a roster for us—for three straight months, though we were relative newcomers, complete strangers turned up at our door, served us and loved on us without any conditions or intrusive questions. They simply lavished meals and help on us during a time when we could hardly see a way forward. Those warm-hearted people oozed the unconditional love of God. This touched me deeply—and became a seed that would, later on, lead to the birthing of 'Nourish Gardens' as I experienced first-hand what it was like to receive when I had no way of giving back.

Now I remembered the promise God had given me as a young adult way back in the little old church: *'When you pass through the waters, I will be with you, and when you pass through the rivers, they will not sweep over you. When you walk through the fire, you will not be burned; the flames will not set you ablaze . . . because I love you.'* 'There it is,' I thought. What I dismissed as a young person was finally coming to pass. I was travelling through troubled waters, but I was going to be okay. *'God is real,'* I was assured of that. *'I trust in him. He has promised to take care of me because I am precious in his sight and he loves me.'*

THE LEARNING CURVE

While I was working, Jimmy was busy trying to recover. The specialist had suggested that he lay down in a darkened room for two, one-hour sessions every day for the first eight weeks, which he did religiously though it nearly drove him insane. Suddenly he went from being a workaholic to not being able to do a single thing. Just lying down in a room was hard-going for him. In fact, he got quite low in his spirit, but he kept it up because he really did want to get well. The theory behind the rest was that he needed to give his brain a break from all stimuli. While his brain was activated, it was working, and therefore could not heal. To recover at all, Jimmy's brain needed to be in a state of complete rest.

During that time, we learned a lot about head injuries and how people with head injuries cannot cope with sensory overload. 'Think of a sensory lasagna,' someone explained to us. 'If you are talking to Jimmy, that's one layer of sensory input, but if you then start to wave your arms around while you talk, that becomes another layer. If the radio is on in the background, that's another layer added in, and if the children are bouncing on the trampoline in the background, that's another sensory layer. Factor in having a television on, or a clock ticking; all it might take, then, to fully stack the lasagna, would be for you to tap your fingers on a mug you are holding, for example, and it's enough to send Jimmy into sensory overload.' Now I could see—all those layers of noise and movement in combination caused Jimmy to escalate extremely quickly, primarily because the part of his brain that was most damaged was his frontal lobe.

When someone without a head injury gets upset, the feeling usually brews slowly enough that they can talk themselves down, control their response, and keep themselves from completely overreacting. With head injury patients, however, any provocation can cause them to 'blow a fuse' and it might only take a second or so—there is no lag time allowing a person to calm down or take stock. So, if Jimmy *felt* mad, he *was* mad! That is how he would operate.

We were told there was a window of about two years, post injury, for a blueprint to form for life. During this time, a patient could work at repairing the brain damage to a point; some even went ahead in leaps and bounds—but outside of that timeframe, the outcome was usually set in concrete. Whatever the progress had been to that point, that would be how it would look for the rest of their life. Unfortunately for us, it had been well over eight years since Jimmy had been injured. We had lost that vital window of time. On top of that, we now realised, Jimmy had actually ended up with a second head injury when he went into the coma.

There are two ways to receive a head injury—one is by receiving a blunt force to the head, and the other is through a lack of oxygen to the brain. Jimmy, in fact had encountered both, on two different occasions. 'When you receive one injury on top of another,' the specialist told us, 'you get a compound effect, which magnifies the effects of the original injury tenfold.' The doctors likened the symptoms of a patient who goes untreated, to the analogy of a frog. When you put it in water and turn up the heat, the water slowly gets hotter, but the frog gets so used to the temperature that it doesn't realise that it is actually cooking to death, and eventually it dies. 'Over time, the symptoms will slowly get worse,' we were told. 'And as a family you get so conditioned to accommodating that person, that you get to a point where it is out of control but you don't even realise how bad it is, until it's too late.'

That was certainly a true description of what was happening to us as a family. I knew I wasn't well, that I wasn't coping, and that things weren't right. The agitation had been building in our home year after year, yet still I could not understand how Jimmy could be so grumpy. At celebrations like birthdays and Christmas, he would sit in the corner of the room like a grumpy old man with his arms folded and his eyes closed. Now I realised that those were the worst times for him—that he was in complete sensory overload, and though he did not even know what he was doing, he was intuitively giving himself what he needed. He needed to close his eyes to shut out the overwhelming environment around him.

When you find yourself in your darkest, most despairing moments, you have a choice—it's fight, or flight. You either believe that God is for you, or that God is absent. I have always believed that God is for me and that he is with me, and therefore, my response was to run towards the Lord as hard as I could and to press into him with all my might. That was all that was left for me to do. I had nothing else. I was stripped bare of all my emotional, physical and psychological strength, and all I could do was to completely surrender to him and his will for my life. When I hit complete darkness, I simply pressed into him; I cried out to him. In my most raw moments, I was able to be completely honest with my grief and my sense of overwhelm.

Jimmy and I mourned the years that we had lost together—seven years where we had suffered as a family and endured so much. I grieved the times when Jimmy had not been able to join in with us at family events or to just be there as a dad. I grieved for all the desires I had held in my heart for our family. Together, we grieved it all. The man I had met all those years earlier was tenderhearted and gentle; although he was always strong in personality, he also carried a soft side. Now, we had to let go of all our expectations and accept the man Jimmy had become. I wrote this poem as I began to process my loss:

MEETING YOU

We started out, you and me, two carefree lovebirds,
I, in love . . . and you, with me.
Such life, such gain.
I never thought I would find just the one . . . all mine.
You knew me well, you loved me deeply,
We became as one and started on life's journey hand in hand.
I will never forget the man I met.

Then, in one bitter night, life's cruel hand
Took you away blow by blow.
Life left you, and I tried to find you.
Invisible shrapnel, all amuck,
Lights turned off, destruction around you,
We couldn't see, we'd lost our way,
I couldn't find you—this love of mine

I lost you, I lost you, love of mine.
I will never forget the man I met.
I'm learning to love again, I've said my goodbyes.
Each day set before me, I stumble and try—so this is
what it means
to truly love one another in sickness and in health,
not wanting, but for the other.

I'm sorry I'm not perfect.
All I can do is try to stand beside you
and get to know . . . the man I've now met.
Love of mine,
love of mine.

NEW GRIEF

Just as we were adjusting to the separation in our marriage, another separation occurred, one which caused me great grief. Years earlier my dad had been diagnosed with cancer. He had battled it bravely for many years, but now, he became gravely ill. The cancer had spread, and the prognosis was not looking good. Trying to settle his affairs, my dad came to ask Jimmy and me for financial help. Wanting to do what we could, Jimmy and I decided to put our plans to build on hold, in order to help my parents financially through this difficult time. Sadly, however, this brought only pain, confusion and grief to us all. I began waking in the night in a cold sweat, wondering if we would ever be able to make peace. It was one of the most painful experiences I have ever walked through in my life. On top of the turmoil with Jimmy, and knowing that my dad did not have long to live, we were now also estranged from my parents.

GLIMMERS OF HOPE

During this time, Jimmy and I kept trying to put things back together. Although we were separated, we would sit side by side, looking back over photo albums and reminiscing about the good things that had brought us together. We wanted to remind ourselves that we had a history together, that we had a life and a wonderful family, and so we poured over our wedding album and photographs from when the children were young, reminding ourselves that we should not take it all for granted, that we were worth fighting for. It was a healing and positive step forward for us, and helped us as we began to look ahead and not behind.

We even started to date again, just Jimmy and I, going out together, almost as if we were starting from scratch. I was getting to know the new Jimmy. Our pastor had given us a rule which I found especially helpful—that when we were on dates, we weren't allowed to try and fix anything, or talk about our 'issues,' but to make those dates a time where we built new memories together, positive happy memories. The goal was just to be in the present, enjoying the moment—and it worked. We were starting to move forward.

Around this time, my youngest son received his 'supernatural moment,' just as I had prayed all my children would. He was sitting at the dinner table one day with my daughter and I, grappling with the concept of how Jesus, a man, could get into a person's heart. 'How does he fit in, though?' he asked. He held his fingers a little way apart and placed them over his heart as if to measure how a man might fit inside. As best as I could, I tried to explain that Jesus was also a spirit, like the air that we breathe, and that we could indeed ask him to come into our hearts and be like our best friend. My son sat there and pondered awhile, and then said, 'I want to do that right now!' Together, we prayed, and he asked Jesus to get right on in there and be part of his life! The moment he did this, both he and his sister got completely filled with the joy of the Lord. They started to jump around the room and were so excited.

Eventually, they sat back down and I began to play a funny game with them both. Taking a banana sticker, I placed it on my nose and carried on talking to them as if nothing was on my face. 'Mum!' my son would say, 'there's a sticker on your nose!' 'What?' I said, 'no there isn't . . . oh, look over there'—and as I pointed behind their backs, I quickly switched the sticker to my eyelid. Then they would turn back squeal and laugh and tell me I had a sticker on my eyelid now! And so the game went on.

Several turns later my little boy shot back and looked at me wide eyed. 'What was that?' he said. 'What?' I replied. 'That bright light that went across the room,' he replied. I was looking at the same time and I hadn't see anything. 'How big was it?' I asked. 'It was taller than the door and it went right through it! It shot past the fireplace and out that other door!' he exclaimed. 'Wow,' I told him, 'I think you have just seen an angel!' But my young son was perplexed. 'Why didn't you see it?' he asked. 'Well,' I replied. 'I think God chose to reveal himself especially to you. First you believed without seeing and then he blessed you by letting you see something you could believe in,' I said. 'It was something very special he chose to do just for you.'

Our pastor came to pray a blessing through the house we were living in at that time, and I recall that when he reached the loungeroom with the fireplace in it, he said, 'I believe someone is going to see an angel in this room.' Well, from that moment on, I took to having my devotional times in that room every day, praying with one of my eyes half open, waiting for my angelic visit! 'Lucky little boy,' I thought to myself.

These encounters occurred during some of the most difficult times in our lives and taught me without a doubt that God walks beside us, he never abandons us, and he is very near to those that call on him.

I also quickly learned that the children also needed to be children and that although we were looking after Jimmy, we needed to look after their needs as well. I tried to give them times when they could have fun and not feel that they had to walk around quietly on tiptoes. To help with that, we made a rule that they could have their friends over to play and be as loud and boisterous as they wanted to be, until five p.m., when Jimmy came home from work. This gave them a chance to play music and run around and do crazy things—to let their hair down a little bit. After five p.m., the focus would be on 'looking after dad,' by doing quiet activities instead. Somehow, we were trying to strike a balance between accommodating Jimmy's need for a peaceful and quiet atmosphere, while still looking after our needs as a family. If we could just maintain this way of life, perhaps we could all stay healthy and sane.

The other thing I made sure to do, was to encourage the kids not to take things personally. I explained that we still loved Jimmy, that we loved dad and that dad dearly loved them as his children. I tried to help them learn to separate out Jimmy's sickness from who he was as their dad, and so, whenever he had an outburst, I would say that he was having an 'Uncle George moment.' I would say, 'Oh, mad Uncle George'—and that was their cue that dad wasn't himself, it was just dad when he was not well. It helped them understand that it was his head injury that was doing the speaking and the acting out, not the real Jimmy, and it helped the kids to not take things so personally. It has also helped them to develop empathy and to deepen their character to the point where they were able to love and care for him as a dad who had needs in the family as well. The reality was, though, that there were many times when, as a mother, I found it absolutely heartbreaking to watch as my kids struggled to cope with the carnage.

PROVISION

The short term rental house we were in ended up being placed on the market for sale, meaning that we were able to stay there a lot longer than we expected—at least a year or so—but also that we had to vacate the house every Sunday while the agent held open homes. It was becoming tiresome, getting the house spruced up week by week (cleaning was certainly not my forte!) then having to find something to do for the day while the open home was happening.

I decided that we should think about finding somewhere else to live. I prayed to the Lord and began thinking about what we might need. It was very early days with learning to manage Jimmy's head injury and he was still very fragile. I knew that moving house in itself would be highly stressful, and thought to myself, 'Oh, Lord. I don't want this to be a difficult move.'

One day, I was standing at the window looking across the fence at the cute little house next door. It was very quaint, almost like a doll's house. 'Gosh, that's a lovely house,' I thought. I knew it was a rental property and suddenly found myself thinking, 'I'd really like to live in that place. That would be awesome—but then again, there are people living there, and I can't exactly knock on their door and say, "Hi, are you thinking of moving out, because I'd like to rent this place?!"'

I continued the mental dialogue about our needs. *We need at least four bedrooms, and we need a very soundproof home, with two living areas, so Jimmy can have peace and quiet in one loungeroom, while the kids can be noisy in the other. We also need a place where Jimmy can store his tools.* I'd done the math and knew that the best we could pay was four hundred and fifty dollars a week, and with that, I left my thoughts hanging, hopeful and trusting.

The very next day, before I had even asked or prayed, as was often the way, God provided. Looking on a real estate website, I couldn't believe my eyes. It appeared the house next door had just popped up as a new listing—and, it was advertised at four hundred and fifty dollars per week! The photo was taken from an unusual angle, though; I wasn't one hundred percent sure if it really was 'my house,' so I called my eldest son and asked him to take a quick look for me. That night, he sneaked around with his torch, and soon returned. 'Yes, mum' he said, excitedly, 'that is the house that is for rent!'

So, we put in our application—and soon discovered that the house next door had everything that was on our family wish list. Suddenly, a conversation between Jimmy and I came back to me. 'What if this house sells, Cindy?' he had asked. 'What will we do then?' 'I can tell you,' I had assured him, 'the house will not sell until the Lord has a new place for us to move into.' Now I almost felt sorry for the couple who had been trying to sell our house. The Lord's hand was with us, and there was no way he would let the house sell until he had lined up a place for us first and provided for our needs. I was just so filled with faith on that matter!

Jimmy had persisted, however. 'Okay, Cindy, I know you have your heart set on that house next door, but what if we don't get it? Then what are we going to do?' 'But we will!' I insisted, 'We will get that house! That house has been set aside for us. It is our place and we will be moving into it.' I was emphatic on that point. 'That's all very well,' retorted Jimmy, 'but what if we don't get it?' Again, I simply looked at him, and with no question in my mind, said, 'but we will.'

Sure enough, the Lord allowed us to secure the house next door, and before long, it was a done deal. On moving day, friends and family again rallied to help us move. Jimmy had friends who helped him as he pottered away quietly in the shed packing his tools, while the kids literally picked up their beds and walked them right next door, still fully assembled! That day, we were able to simply carry all of our furniture into our new home. It was one of the easiest moves we had ever done. The manner of God's provision for us as a family was amazing. He just knew exactly what we needed and exactly when we needed it.

As we returned the key to our previous landlord at the end of the day, however, my thoughts were on the fact that I believed the house would not sell until we had found another place to move into. Now, curiosity got the better of me. 'Incidentally,' I asked as we were about to say goodbye, 'how are you getting on with selling the house? Have you found a buyer for your property yet?' 'Funny you should ask,' she replied. 'Actually, we sold the house today! I've just come back from signing the papers.' 'Isn't God's timing amazing?' I thought. What were the chances of that happening? For over a year, the house had not sold, and now, on the very day that our tenancy finished and we moved out, a sale went through. 'God, your timing is impeccable,' I prayed. 'You orchestrate things so beautifully. You care for me so deeply and take care of all our needs.' I was reminded of the scripture in Psalm 37:4 *Delight yourself in the Lord and he will give you the desires of your heart.*

That house ended up being the most soundproof house I had ever lived in. You could be literally yelling in one room and not even hear it from the room beneath! It was the perfect house for Jimmy's needs. It was also a great place for the kids. Now they had a rumpus room where they could unravel a little bit and make as much noise as they liked. Not only that, but the home was a beautiful character-cottage, set on ten acres. I had always hankered for a place with a country setting and space for the kids to run wild and free. In the yard, they could build tree huts, explore the land, and fish for eels.

The property was also full of fruit trees . . . once again, we were blessed with an abundance of citrus fruit, peaches, plums, and feijoa. It was just a wonderful little place to live! I was always impressed with how the Lord had given us a place to enjoy while we waited to build on our own land. He had seen to it that we were not cooped up in a little townhouse, but were in a wide open place. It was a continual reminder that he would provide all our needs and make our paths straight as we continued to follow him.

RECONCILED

It was at this time that God also poured out his grace between me and my dad. I loved my dad so much, yet for two years, as he battled with sickness, we had been estranged. Now, however, forgiveness came. Thankfully, I was able to nurse him in the last few weeks of his life; he even asked me to sing at his funeral.

HE HOLDS THE 'TRUMP CARD'

I am so thankful for the way God always walked beside me, giving me firm convictions and peace in the midst of the storms. There was so much going on all at once, so much to work through. Before long, we received notification that the roads authority wanted to expand the motorway near the land we had previously purchased. Our property, we were informed, was required in order to carry out their plans, and the process of negotiating with all the landowners along the motorway had begun. We were told that both the roads authority and us, as property owners, needed to obtain an independent valuation of the land, and that after agreeing to meet in the middle, we would be paid out for the agreed price. The only problem was, that we put forward an honest valuation and they simply did not. Their official valuation was well below what the property was worth—and they knew it. I could not believe it. It felt like daylight robbery and that they were a bunch of crooks. I felt sorry for all the other homeowners who were also getting ripped off. This was our investment, a property that we did not intend on selling in the near future. Our intention had been to subdivide and thereby maximise its full value at a later date.

When we refused to sell, the wrangle was set to continue for the long haul, but we were determined to hold our ground. Even after the earthworks began, flattening the ground all around us and demolishing the houses on either side of our land, our little property still stood strong! I would drive along the motorway, see our two houses and think, 'oh my goodness, we are the ones holding up all this progress!'

Around this time the Lord gave Jimmy a dream in which he and I were driving around in the back of a van with a bunch of guys in balaclavas; we could not see their faces. Around and around in circles we went, getting nowhere. Eventually the men threw us out on the side of the curb beside a rolling green paddock. They also threw a wooden chest in our direction, and then drove off. When we opened the chest, it was full of gold, and we, of course, could not believe it.

The guys wearing balaclavas represented the transit authority. We had never actually met them face to face, as we had only ever dealt with them through lawyers, which explained the balaclavas. Driving in circles represented the fact that we were getting nowhere with them, even after two years of negotiating. The paddock was our land, we believed, and the gold represented the payout we should expect from the government authority, which we were going to need for our building project.

The dream encouraged us to hold fast and steady, and assured us that everything would eventually work in our favour. Finally, we received a letter from the government lawyer, effectively saying, 'name your price and we will give it to you!' At that point, I could have named a hefty price, but then I would have been just as guilty as them. I did not want to rip anyone off. I just wanted what was fair and equitable. I wanted the true value of the property. Over the past two years, however, the value of our property had risen by a whopping seventy percent.

Soon, the deal was done. That little property I had purchased by the motorway, the property that my dad had raised his eyebrows over, had become a very valuable piece of land. God already knew this, of course; he had his hand all over it, even when I 'just had a sense' all those years ago, that this property was for me. Taking care to seek him out at every turn in our lives and to listen to his ever-so-subtle promptings had become an invaluable way of living.

Looking back, I often think that yes, things were definitely not great, but still the Lord was so gracious and kind to us. We were walking through the fire and through the valleys; at times were very desperate, it felt dark, and we got terribly low. But through it all, the Lord walked beside us, ready to birth in us a new vision, a plan and a desire that we had never had before.

fresh vision

OUR LAND

For more than seven years we had been looking for another piece of land to purchase—a property where we could finally build a home for our family, as well as begin to cultivate the incredible vision God had given us along the way, yet nothing quite seemed to tick all the boxes.

Still, I would drag Jimmy along to each and every new piece of bare land that popped up on the market. Generally, he would arrive, take a quick look around, say, 'No, this is not the one,' and then we would leave. That's how the drill went, so I decided to look further abroad at neighbouring pockets of rural land since we were having no luck in our immediate area. Again, we had our wish list. We were looking for about five acres. It needed to have its own driveway with a nice flat area for building, a rural sweeping view with trees not too close to the house site so as to avoid clogged drainage pipes. I longed for a nice established shady tree, one that we could attach a swing to and enjoy a meal under its canopy.

Clearly, Jimmy was the practical one and I was the dreamer, the visionary, the idealist. It was always form versus function with us two. But we settled on the details. The land needed to be fairly close to town but close enough that the kids could ride their bikes to school if they needed to. *Not too much to ask*, we thought. *Oh, and a sunny aspect with no neighbours looking in on us*, since I valued my privacy.

One day a beautiful section came up for sale and we went to take a look. Jimmy had been standing on the property less than a minute when he looked around and simply said, 'Yep.' I nearly fell over backwards! 'What did you say?' I asked. 'Yep, this is the one,' he replied. Jimmy knew without a shadow of a doubt that this was the property. I was so excited that I couldn't believe it. Finally, after seven years, we were in agreement. We had found a property that ticked all the boxes—every single one, right down to the big established shady tree that sat squarely in the middle of the section!

The land was stunning, with alpacas grazing on it, but it turned out to be a tricky piece of land, full of covenants and council requirements that we were going to have to wade through in order to build. But it could be worth it, we thought. The real estate agent, however, turned out to be a rather smooth talker; we didn't like his slick lines or his pushy approach to selling. Soon, we were feeling uncomfortable with the whole process. Was it really worth all the hassle, or not? We were of two minds. Then, that same week, an old school friend of mine who was living in Australia called me out of the blue. It had been a long time since we had caught up, and she had no idea of what we were doing, but what she said had a profound effect on us.

'Look,' she said, 'I had a dream about you guys last night and have been unable to get it out of my head, so I thought I would give you a call. It might be nothing, but at least I'll have it off my chest. It might mean something to you.' I was listening intently by now. My friend continued, 'I dreamed that you had bought a piece of land and placed a large building on it. There was a half built kitchen, and people all around you on the property . . . and I saw alpacas in the paddocks!'

That was all the confirmation we needed to push ahead with the deal. For years after that, it seemed, we waded through permit requirements, house plans, and endless meetings with the council, who always seemed to come up with new hoops to jump through. There were challenges at every corner—all throughout the time when we were in the tiny garage, then the short term rental, and finally, across our time in the quaint cottage next door that we had moved into.

LIVING THE DREAM

When we finally began the excavations, there was a great sense of excitement, a buzz all around! It was official! We could start building. We decided to build the barn and live in it first, then move onto building the main house later on. It was a two story design—Jimmy's workshop was going to be downstairs, and the upstairs would be our home. The barn was expansive, five hundred square metres in total, but Jimmy had a way of finding deals and doing everything on the cheap. He was going to build it on his own and save a fortune, he reckoned.

We had a friend who came along and worked with Jimmy. He was an absolute pro on the digger, and a real hard case. He looked like he came from the rough side of town, with his black clothes and long beard, but he held a deep passion for the Lord. He also loved a challenge. We were digging into the side of the hill, preparing the site for the concrete foundation one day, when the digger lost one of its tracks. That didn't deter our friend one bit. He hobbled along, using the digger arm like a second track. The more challenging it became, the more excited Jimmy and his friend seemed to get about the project. Although we had wanted to build on the flat, the council ended up asking us to shift the barn site onto the side of the hill. This required truckloads of earthworks and excavation. When we eventually poured the concrete foundation, it was a momentous day, for sure.

Jimmy set to work and built all the framing on his own, and when it came time to lift the walls up and into their place, we had a good old fashioned 'barn raising.' Next, the whopping big wooden beams that were two stories high needed to be hoisted up into place. Jimmy thrived on each and every challenge. He figured out a way to hoist the beams into place using just the two of us. We would carry the beams into position one at a time and lay them flat on the concrete pad. *Does he think I am Superwoman?* I often wondered, but Jimmy just carried on, rigging up a boat wrench on top of the wooden framed walls and running the wire down to the beam below. All I had to do, he said, was simply hold the beam and balance it into position while he wound up the wrench. The whole setup looked incredibly dodgy, and I had my doubts, but lo and behold, it worked.

Slowly, the outside of the barn came together, the roofing iron went on and we decided to have a roof shout with all our friends. The night before the celebration, however, the wind picked up and whistled through the house, peeling back half of the roofing iron! Jimmy had forgotten to secure the final row of nails. It looked a real sight when our friends all gathered, but we decided to celebrate anyway and fix it later.

By now, we were keen to stop paying rent and get into the barn as quickly as possible. We could live in it and complete it as we went along, we figured. The reality was, of course, that it was never going to be an easy solution. We moved in with no doors, no cladding except for building paper, no lights, no kitchen, no bathroom—and three kids in tow. What in the world were we thinking? I sold it to the kids as 'one big adventure.' On the upside, we did have power to the site and one outside tap with running water. During the summer we would use the hose to shower with, and there was a chemical toilet in the old container shed that we had to run up the hill to use. We set up a camp-style kitchen, leaving dishes to soak in large plastic containers and doing one big washup at the end of each day.

Thankfully, with daylight saving, the summer days were long and sunny. We lived by the daylight, rising with the sun in the morning and going to bed each night when 'the light went down.' It was breezy, but not a bad way to live. We got plenty of sleep and maintained very good health; I'm sure because we were so well rested, we never seemed to get too run down.

As the winter approached, however, things became slightly more challenging. We moved the chemical toilet into the barn downstairs and began boiling the kettle for showers, using a facecloth and soap to wipe our bodies down. It was freezing as we stood, stark naked, on the concrete pad, performing our extremely quick bathing ritual. We ate dinner by candlelight each night—and that was lovely. Upstairs, the outside cladding was still in progress. We had no internal walls. It was just one expanse of space. We lived marae-style, with our beds all scattered and spread out everywhere. I even set up a four-metre-high teepee inside the barn. This became a changing room and a place to get away from everyone else when we needed a bit of peace and privacy.

The nights soon began to get dark earlier, and so we bought everyone a headlamp. We would all walk around upstairs at night with these little lamps on our heads, looking like a bunch of fireflies hovering around and darting from here to there. For the most part, as soon as we had finished dinner, we all jumped into our beds to read, because it was just too freezing to be anywhere other than tucked up under the warm covers. I had layered the children's beds with five or six blankets, just to keep them warm, and still their breath rose like smoky vapours into midair each night. Yes, it really was that cold! Our youngest son had asthmatic symptoms during the winter months and I realised that the way we were living was not conducive to a healthy way of living. Needing to problem solve, I came up with the idea of setting him up in a pup tent inside the barn. That way he could breathe in the circulated warm air. It worked well . . . until the coldest months kicked in. Then, no matter what we did, the kids were cold, and there was no way to heat the barn.

Soon, I had another idea—we borrowed a caravan, wrapped it with the insulation that we were going to use for the house, and parked it downstairs, inside the barn. That night, we moved all three of the kids into the caravan where they could be toasty and warm. I felt so much happier knowing that they were comfortable. *Roommates,* I thought, *how much fun!* As I cooked dinner each night, the kids would often be scooting past me in the 'kitchen' on their skateboards and rollerblades while dancing to music. 'What a life!' I told myself, 'we are living the dream.' It was crazy, for sure, and extreme at times, but somehow it appealed to my sense of adventure. Most of the time, the kids also coped well, and were always so good natured about everything.

Eventually we got the cladding wrapped around the house, and a friend who was a builder insisted that a bathroom needed to be built for the family, and volunteered to help Jimmy get the job done. Six months after we moved in, we had a hot running shower! I will never forget turning that shower on for the first time. It took appreciation to a whole new level for me.

Now it was time to build the internal walls, and so, we moved everything over to one end of the barn, until we were concertinered together down at the far end. The bedrooms were going in. We aimed to get the job done by Christmas and decided that we would give the kids an 'extreme makeover and grand room reveal' for their Christmas presents. I worked on making their individual bedroom spaces magical and could not wait to see them settle into their new rooms.

As the momentum built, I asked our son, 'what are you looking forward to most about your new room?' It was the night before Christmas. Laying back in his bed, he put his arms behind his head and sighed. 'Four walls,' he simply said. I chuckled and asked him again. 'Okay, and what else?' 'A light!' he replied. Our three children had become the most grateful kids in the world; they never took anything for granted.

After Christmas, we moved fully into the finished side of the barn, where it was easier to heat the rooms now that we had insulation in the walls. It was bliss! The other end of the barn was to remain an open plan living area with a kitchen and dining space all in one. Two years after we moved in, I had finally had an upstairs kitchen with a dishwasher and running hot water. It was wonderful.

NOURISH

While we were building the barn, the Lord began to give me a larger vision for our land. I shared my dream with Jimmy: *A beautiful vegetable garden, with fruit trees, and honey to share in abundance with others—a place to paint and explore.* Having been through so much, I had found a desire within me to help others who were going through difficult times. I wanted them to know that they were not alone, that we could journey through life together. I wanted to encourage them and build them up, and I wanted them to experience the tangible touch of the Lord in their lives through practically giving to them in their times of need. I felt so drawn to the idea of going back to basics, connecting with the earth, growing healthy, organic food on our land that would, in turn, nourish those around us. I wanted to serve those who had no capacity to give back, to show them the love of Jesus. I dreamed of a haven where people could feel the presence of the Lord, enjoy rest and peace, and find a loving, listening ear. It was so new, so fresh! This vision seemed to come out of nowhere. It was certainly not what I had planned for our land. I had dreamed of a place where our children would grow up and build happy memories. However, God had bigger plans, and I was starting to get excited.

CONFIRMATION

Jimmy slowly warmed to the idea, but at times I struggled to talk with him. 'Lord,' I said. 'He's not much of a talker. Can you speak to him? I don't know how . . . perhaps through dreams and visions?' That very week, I got woken up in the dead of night. 'Cindy, Cindy, wake up!' Jimmy was saying. 'I've had a dream! Go and put the kettle on and let's have a cup of tea.'

Once we were awake and comfortable, Jimmy began to share his dream with me. *I was dead*, he said. *It was my funeral service. There was a chisel sitting on top of my casket, and I was seeing it all from a bird's-eye view. Then, the next minute, I was standing on our land, and as I looked down the hill there were these magnificent horses, and ghost-like riders were doing incredible tricks on them, jumping on and off, and around them. It was amazing to watch! They rode up the hill, and as they approached, I could see that their clothes were disintegrating and see-through, as if they were spiritual beings. There were three of them. They rode up to me and stopped. When they looked at me, it was as if they could see right into my soul and into my very being. One of them said to the other, 'he's one of us' and the other joked 'yeah, but he's not much of a talker!'*

At that point, I smiled to myself. This was, indeed, confirmation that God had answered my prayer—he had put that line in there just for me! Then Jimmy went on, *The beings said to me, 'We're sending you a team—and they're a great team.' At that very moment a herd of horses jumped the lower fence and came galloping up the hill and stopped in front of me. I looked at the horses and said, 'I don't even like horses! I can't get on one of those. Just then a baby horse came through the herd and I laughed.*

I got the interpretation of the dream straight away. It was a commissioning dream. The casket represented Jimmy's old self; the chisel, his day job as a builder. God was calling him into something new, into ministry. 'Forget the former things,' the Lord was saying. The spiritual beings were representative of this—it was time to operate in the spiritual, to focus on God's plans and purposes. The horses represented something totally different, something new and out of Jimmy's comfort zone. *Gardening and growing food!* I suddenly thought. We were certainly not gardeners but the Lord was going to put a team of people around us to help us complete the task. The baby horse represented how we were going to grow and learn from others, taking one baby step at a time, and at a pace that we could manage.

How incredible and significant that God gave the commissioning dream to Jimmy and not me. Little did we know that within weeks of this dream, our first team member would arrive.

MARIAN

I was at a church function when I found myself sharing my vision with the woman beside me. Marian was a short, Dutch lady in her fifties, with cropped, grey hair. The following week, she came over to speak with me. I recall the strange feeling I had as I almost peered down at her. Our height difference was so huge! But Marian looked up and said, 'I'm really interested in what you're doing.' 'That's nice,' I replied, 'thank you.' The next week, the same thing happened. Again, I responded, 'Yes, that's nice. Thank you.' On the third week, her husband also pitched in. 'My wife is very interested in what you are doing.' 'Yes, I heard, that's nice, thank you,' I told him.

Finally, Marian came to me the following week. 'Look, Cindy, I've left my job *and I am interested in what you are doing.*' 'Wow,' I thought. 'She has left her paid job to come and volunteer with me in the garden fulltime!' 'But I'm not ready,' I replied in shock. But God, it seemed, was getting this thing going whether I was ready or not, and Marian was the perfect person to help me turn the vision into a reality. Not long after, I left my teaching job, and together we began working, talking and praying about what we felt the Lord wanted us to do at Nourish.

I was soon to discover that I had found gold in this woman. Marian became one of the most incredible people I have ever met or had the privilege of working alongside. Her faithfulness, humility, hard work and love melted my heart. My character and faith grew because of what I observed in her every thought, word and deed. She taught me so much. The first task we decided to tackle was to clear the boundaries of any potential hazards such as large trees that might fall onto the garden, and to get rid of any weeds that could spread and potentially take over. The whole area was thick with weeds; there was gorse the size of trees, rambling thicket-like vines that could not be passed through, and privet which was growing its own little forest. At times it was hard to see where any of the lovely New Zealand natives were amongst it all.

It was a big task, but necessary in more ways than just one. Marian and I met three days a week to slash, saw, and pull out weeds, and as we did, we got to know one another and had the chance to brainstorm ideas about how the vision of the garden could unfold in a practical way. Soon, the 'Nourish Garden' vision became clear. I wrote it out on a blackboard, where all of us could be reminded as we came together:

"We aim to grow organic produce to help support families in need. We work together with those interested in gardening, serving practically, or those suffering from depression, loneliness, trauma, etc. who are looking to find healing through friendship, fresh air and exercise, giving back to others and ultimately, experiencing the love of Jesus in their lives."

'LOST' LOUISE

A few months into the project, Marian and I had a conversation. 'Wouldn't it be great,' we thought, 'if we could build up a core team of gardeners who were also interested in pastoral care—people who could work alongside others who were in need of support.'

At the time, we were looking for native plants to place along our boundaries, and one day, Marian decided it was time to purchase some basic tools. Off we set to the hardware store, but all along the way, my mind was on a woman I knew who had recently retired and loved gardening. Who would have guessed, that as we entered the automated doors of the hardware store, we would nearly bump into that very woman! There, not even a metre from us, stood Louise! 'Wow, Louise' I said, 'What are you doing here?' 'Oh' she replied, sounding slightly miffed. 'I was driving around looking for this garden club that I was going to join, but I ended up getting lost, so I thought, "Oh, bother. I'll just go to the hardware store instead."'

'Well, welcome to your new gardening club!' I said with a cheeky grin on my face. 'Can I buy you a coffee?' Together we sat down, and I shared our vision with her. I asked her what she used to do before her retirement, and she mentioned that she had been a doctor who specialised in mental health. 'Wow,' I thought. 'Just what we need!' I then asked her about her garden. 'Well,' she said, 'I've got a whole lot of native plants that are a real nuisance. I need to get rid of them all!' And so, our team began to grow.

ANSWERED PRAYERS

The garden was set on an acre of land on a sloping section just below the barn where we lived. It was a big vision, and I wanted to maximise the productivity of the land in order to serve as many people as we were able to. With a big vision, however, came an enormous need for resources to keep it going. We were going to need mulch, compost, plants, tools . . . and so much more. And though our little team was happy to fund and resource it ourselves, God, as it turned out, had other plans.

NATIVE TREES

We had a council requirement on our land that meant we had to regenerate certain parts of our land as part of our resource consent requirement. There was a deadline to complete the planting schedule, and as it was approaching fast, Marian bought it up in conversation. I had been putting it off, because the truth was, I simply did not want to spend all our money purchasing native trees to satisfy council requirements when I would rather be investing our funds into buying plants for our garden.

That afternoon, my husband came down to the paddock where we were working to see how we were doing. 'How many trees do we need to plant in the designated area?' I asked. 'About seven hundred,' he replied. I went away and pondered the matter, and the next morning I prayed, 'Lord, I need seven hundred native trees free of charge by the end of today.' My faith was confident and unwavering, and as I drove the kids to school and wandered into the grounds, I happened to bump into a friend who had a mutual interest in gardening. 'Hey, Camilla,' I said, 'you don't happen to know where I could get a hold of some native trees, do you?'

Her reply turned out to be just the answer I needed. 'I think the school has an incentive running,' she said. 'They grow native trees here with the children, and then, when the trees are mature enough, they go and plant them out on local farms. If you talk to Lucy, she might be able to help you out.' Having taught at the school for ten years, I was familiar with the staff and they knew me well. 'Hey, Lucy,' I said when I saw she had a moment. 'You don't happen to know where I can get a hold of some native trees, do you?' 'Oh yes,' she rolled her eyes and seemed rather disgruntled. 'I've got a whole lot of natives and no one to give them to. The farmer who was going to take them has just pulled out!' 'I'll take them all,' I said. 'Yeah, but the problem is that there's so much red tape involved,' she replied. 'I can't give them to you because now they all have to be returned to head office and there's a long queue of farmers waiting in line for trees. In the meantime, I'm stuck with them all and they really need to get into the ground straight away before they become root bound. You'll have to ring Gail at head office and see what she says.'

Grabbing her number, I headed home undeterred, called her up, and explained my situation. 'I understand,' Gail said, 'but unfortunately, I cannot give them to you. There is a procedure we need to follow and I'll have to put you on the waiting list. It's about a two-year wait. But I tell you what,' she said. 'I am actually in the area and could come by today for a site assessment if you like.' 'Perfect,' I said.

As we walked around the land, I told her about my long-standing relationship with the primary school and shared the vision of Nourish with her. Soon we came to the area that needed planting. She looked at it thoughtfully and paused awhile. 'Stuff it,' she said, nudging her elbow into me. 'I'll give you all those trees, the labour for planting day and the tools you will need. You'll just have to provide lunch on planting day. How does that sound?'

I was elated. Grinning from ear to ear, I couldn't help but stand in awe of God. Not only had he given me seven hundred native trees for free by the end of the day, but he had also provided the tools and labour! God had outdone himself. *Over and above*, I thought. I was beginning to see how big he really is and how easily we limit him and what he can do for us, how we tend to pray little prayers because we put him in such a little box. If we are doing things that please him, however, things that are dear to his heart, then he will certainly resource and equip us to carry out the tasks he has given us to do. 'Seek first the kingdom of God, and all these things shall be added unto you[4],' the Bible says. What a day! I was on a high!

I began to pray bold, full-of-faith prayers, knowing that when I went to the local community to ask for resources for Nourish, I was not asking for myself, but rather for my God. I was his ambassador, and this was his vision. He wanted this thing to succeed—I just had the exciting privilege of being a part of it. I was reminded of the scripture which says, 'You do not have because you do not ask.'[5]

---

4   Matthew 6:33

5   James 4:2

It was important for me to reflect his very nature through everything we did. I wanted the best of the best for the people we were to serve. *After all, God doesn't give leftovers. He lavishes on us and gave us his very best, even His one and only son, Jesus. He let him die so that we might live. There is no greater gift that he could have bestowed on us.* It got me thinking. 'If we were to reflect who he was, then we would need the best soil in order to grow the best produce. Every component required for good compost will need to be the best of the best. The food will need to be full of nutrients and generous in proportions.'

I felt the Lord's pleasure as I pondered this fact. It was like he was saying, 'Yeah, girl! Now you're getting it.' I cannot tell you how excited I became about praying—and, the answers to our prayers started coming in thick and fast. Soon I began to pray, 'Lord, give us another answered prayer so that we may brag on you!' This became one of my greatest delights; it was the most exciting adventure, as we wondered what was to be around the next corner. As I began to understand the sheer magnitude, might and grandeur of who God was, my thinking was absolutely transformed.

Nourish became such a joy and delight for me, and we worked on it as a team for the next six years. It was a season of great purpose and productivity. We ran it three days a week during school hours. Volunteers would come and help out in whatever way they were able. We had people from many different churches, and I loved that aspect of the community—we were a bunch of people coming together from all different denominations, races, social backgrounds, ages and abilities, but we were unified as we found common ground. We all loved Jesus and simply wanted to share his love by coming together and serving others. I felt God's absolute pleasure in this fact and was reminded constantly of the scripture that promises that when we dwell together in unity, then the Lord commands a blessing.[6]

We set about our tasks faithfully. There was always something to do. We grew over a hundred fruit trees, and seven, fifty-metre-long vegetable garden beds. We made a firepit, and created a lovely natural amphitheater setting among the native trees, where groups would gather, and a native bush area where people could go for quiet contemplation. Some people really needed a quiet place to just sit and rest, a place to contemplate, to do some journalling, or pray. Others loved to join in with the team, to do something physical. They needed to feel productive; still others just wanted to sit and talk with someone, to be heard, encouraged and prayed for.

I enjoyed the pastoral side of Nourish and felt so connected to the often-painful stories people shared. People who were in need of support came through word of mouth, or from referrals from pastors. They would always receive a supply of fruit and vegetables and some freshly cut flowers, along with a scripture that brought hope. It was my heart's desire to see people receive so much more than practical help. I wanted them to feel truly nourished in body, mind and spirit, and to leave having experienced God's love. I wanted them to know they were connected, and not alone.

While we were still establishing the garden and waiting for the fruit and vegetables to grow, a market garden in South Auckland began donating a massive trailer-load of potatoes and carrots every week. A team of volunteers would turn up every Thursday when it arrived, and together we would bag the vegetables and then distribute around one hundred and fifty bags to people in the community. For the larger tasks, we would get groups coming in for the day to help us, and this worked so well. We had groups of school children, girl guides, sporting teams, and even corporate groups coming to help in the garden.

There was often a question and answer time, and invariably, someone from each group would ask, 'how do you resource this place?' Then my heart would soar, as I began to tell how we prayed and simply asked God for what we needed. I had the privilege of being able to brag on God! You cannot officially 'preach' in many schools and workplaces in our country, but you certainly can answer questions if asked. Some people were perplexed by our motives and could not understand why we never made any money from it but we were often referred to as the 'God garden' by the groups that visited.

DETERIORATING

There was a sense of duplicity for me during this season. While I was enjoying Nourish with every fibre of my being, my home-life continued to be challenging. Stepping out into the garden each day became my solace, my place of refuge where I found strength and encouragement. I never hid the fact that home life was challenging—in fact, I would often say to those who came, 'I don't profess to have it all together. I am just someone who goes through highs and lows like you, and I want to journey alongside you and encourage you to remember that Jesus walks beside us every step of the way.'

People knew things were hard—but they could not know the full extent of the challenges we faced. My life at home had continued to become increasingly intense; we had dealings with the police, shocking and extreme outbursts, and even situations that resulted in hospitilisation. Slowly but surely, our bodies and minds began to manifest significant symptoms of stress as we continued to experience one traumatic event after another at home. Blow by blow the children and I had been wounded in our spirits. It hurt so much and was always undeserved.

It is fair to say that my body gave up long before my will to battle on did. I had begun to shut down, and spent more and more time in bed, unable to get up. Marian and Louise and the team carried on without me, while I lay just metres away, upstairs in the barn with the curtains drawn, distraught, depressed, and completely debilitated. I felt grieved to my core to see the work going on all around me, and yet I could not physically get up and get going. I had become so unwell by this point, that I was spending most of my days lying on the couch, barely able to get up to make meals for the family or spend time with the kids before and after school. Even basic tasks like showering seemed overwhelming for me. Friends and family would call by to drop off meals at times and clean the house for me; they encouraged me to pursue things that might fill me up and help me find healing—things like exploring my creativity, and catching up with good friends.

The reality was, though, that I had good days and bad days. I felt like a bird trying to fly with its feet stuck in the mud. Often, I would hide in my room, watching movies for hours on end, or I would go on shopping sprees, trying to fill the void of my unhappiness.

By this time, I had been married for nearly twenty years to a man who had suffered a traumatic brain injury just four years after our wedding. I had loved my husband in his sickness and taught my three children to do the same, and though life at home was extremely challenging at times, we had navigated the situation by separating the man from his injury. Twenty years in, however, the pain of watching my children suffer so greatly had become unbearable. My family needed every ounce of the little energy I had left to take care of them, but I had nothing left to give. I could almost feel the life blood draining from me.

THE COLLAPSE

Getting out of bed one night, I went into the bathroom and cried out to God. 'Please don't make me choose between my husband and my children,' I pleaded. It felt impossible to care for them both when my husband's behavior was having such a negative impact on the kids—and vice versa. In tremendous internal pain, I collapsed onto the bathroom floor and only managed to get from there to the car so that I could drive myself to the hospital.

At the hospital, the medical staff performed tests but found nothing. I lay on the bed and began to weep uncontrollably. I felt so alone. 'God' I said, 'who will take care of me?' In that moment, a friend came to mind, and right away I sent her a text to say I was at the hospital. When her reply came through, 'I will come and take care of you,' it was as if God himself had answered my cry. When my friend came, she found me hiding under the sheets. We exchanged no words, yet as she simply sat beside me, the look of love on her face touched me deeply. Placing her hand on my arm, she gently cried alongside me.

For the next two weeks, I was bedridden. My mind was in turmoil. 'Lord, I need clarity,' I prayed. As I began to reflect on the state of my family, I realised that all of us were sick in one way or another. We were in a state of complete dysfunction. 'Lord,' I said. 'I have been going to a psychologist for a year and a half now, I'm taking antidepressants. Why am I am still not getting better? Why is my son's health not improving? Lord, I need clarity,' I pleaded again. 'Please show me what is going on.'

That night, an advertisement I had never seen before, popped up on my computer screen. The advertisement was for an audiobook called, 'When Loving Him is Hurting You,'[7] it covered the whole screen, catching my attention, as if to say, 'you need to listen to this book.' In the moment, I looked at the title and laughed, thinking, 'yeah that's about right!' but when the same title popped up again the next day as well, it felt like something hit me in the chest and was trying to get my attention. I had never had an audiobook suggestion pop up on my screen like that before, and it has never happened to me since.

And so, I began listening—and as I did I found myself reeling. It was as if I were listening to my own story. My blood ran cold as I was suddenly confronted with the fact that it was not just the symptoms of my husband's head injury that I was dealing with. What I had also encountered, was emotional abuse.

My heart sank as I reeled with this new information. I had been blind, and suddenly the smoke screen was removed, giving me clarity on the whole situation for the first time. The book I was listening to had been written by a Christian man with over twen-

---

7   https://www.audible.com.au/pd/When-Loving-Him-Is-Hurting-You-Audiobook/B075WYBX7X

ty years' experience of working alongside women in abusive situations—it was thoughtful and wise, and I was strengthened by the way he brought the Lord into every aspect of the topic. At every crossroad, the author had provided opportunities for the husband to seek help. I admired his approach; he did not encourage rushing into quick separation, but approached it instead as the final answer, after 'having done all else.'

As I listened to the book being read and took slow, careful notes, I came to the realization that my relationship was already a long way down the path towards separation. I had been at many crossroads over the years and every time, had asked for change. It was clear now, that I was already at the end of my marriage journey. 'Lord,' I said, 'if this is you speaking to me and you want me to move out, then you are going to have to be abundantly clear about this. I need you to give me signs and wonders because you know that I believe in marriage for life. If you want me to stay, I will stay, and if you want me to go, I will go, but, please Lord, make it so clear to me that I will never regret my decision and never look back.'

To completely surrender my will to the Lord was a very difficult prayer for me. I was agreeing to stay if He wanted me to stay—and if He wanted me to leave, I was completely letting go, trusting God that He knew what was best for me and my family, and that He would take care of our every need. I agonised over the thought that my marriage might be coming to an end. But I was also convinced that God never intended for anyone to live in an abusive marriage, that it is never acceptable to Him—ever!

At the time, the Lord gave me the words of Isaiah 51:

> 'I, even I, am he who comforts you.
> Who are you, that *you fear mortal men,*
> human beings who are but grass,
> that you *forget the Lord your Maker . . .*
> that you *live in constant terror every day*
> *because of the wrath of the oppressor?*
> The cowering prisoners will soon be set free.
> *They will not die* in their dungeons, *nor will they lack bread,*
> For I am the Lord your God.'

Those words spoke to my heart. Now I could see that, in his grace and mercy, the Lord was taking me by the hand and leading me out of my marriage—for good. But how could that be? I had no idea how to proceed, but I knew He loved me, and I trusted him to show me the way. 'Help me, Lord,' I prayed. And then, two things happened.

As I listened to the radio later that week, I heard an advertisement for a conference. 'Women of Courage' was the theme that year—and in the same way the book had leapt out at me, that conference also caught my attention. I knew God was speaking to me, 'Go to that conference—it's important.'

The other thing that happened was that God gave me a dream. In my dream, I saw seven distinct scenes, much like in a movie. I could already see the significance of the first two scenes. The first had been my shopping spree in the motorbike store. It was true—my overspending had got a hold on me. I had splurged time and time again as a coping mechanism, for sure. The second scene was playing out in my life as well. I'd been sitting around for hours on end, watching movies, trying to escape the reality of my situation. But now, even that scene was changing. Things were already in motion, and God had already given me the keys.

The steps I needed to take in order to leave my marriage behind turned out to be exactly as I had seen in my dream—a series of trapdoors that I would need to pass through, one by one. I could see that the Lord had given me the keys so that I could open each door along the way, and that I would arrive successfully on the other side. For now, though, what lay ahead of me seemed impossible. How could the kids and I possibly leave, yet stay safe?

I prayed at every step, seeking the Lord for his counsel, and confided in several trusted Christian professionals who I knew would bring wisdom into my situation. With my husband's increasingly volatile nature and ability to fly off the handle at any minor situation, I could not begin to imagine how he would react if I were to tell him I was leaving. It was decided that a 'safe exit' would be needed so as not to put the children or myself in harm's way. To do that, we would need to leave quietly, with safety as our first priority. This was a hard decision, because I would have rather spared my husband the shock of coming home to find we had gone, and if I could have done it any other way I would have. But the team of health professionals who had helped me over the years agreed that safety had to come first.

Knowing that I did not want to go with my 'tail between my legs,' I had written a list of the things I would need to get done in advance. That list soon became extensive! I also knew that 'leaving well' meant that we needed to take the things we needed and cherished with us. And so, the exit journey began. Now, the trap doors were about to be unlocked in the most amazing ways.

Trapdoor 1: Finances

My first priority was to free up my finances. We had saved up some money to build our home—now I needed to be able to access those funds to withdraw what was rightfully mine. The trouble was, my husband had always managed that part of our finances, and I had no way of knowing the passwords to our savings account. 'Lord, how do you want me to navigate this?' I asked again, trusting Him to help me work out the details.

The next day, He gave me a vision; I saw the Red Sea parting, and through the middle was a carpeted pathway that led up to a bank teller. The words, 'be bold and courageous,' came to me as well. It was as if he was saying to me, 'Go to the bank and ask for what you need.' I was petrified, however, and not knowing too much about our joint account, I wasn't sure if the bank needed my husband's permission to withdraw large amounts of funds from the account. What if they called him to check while I was at the bank? Then what would I do?

In faith, I leaned on the verses the Lord had already given me from Isaiah 51:10: *Was it not you who dried up the sea, the waters of the great deep, who made a road in the depths of the sea so that the redeemed might cross over?* I went to the bank, literally trembling, and feeling weak all over. As I started to walk up the aisle of the bank, my hands were sweaty and I worried that the teller might notice my nerves and get suspicious. Over and over I began to recite the words in my head, 'be bold and courageous in the Lord,' which then turned into speaking in tongues as I neared the counter. Now, the Lord reminded me of another scripture from the same chapter: 'I have put my words in your mouth.' 'Just breathe, Cindy,' I told myself, ' . . . and trust.'

'Hi,' I said when it was my turn to speak with the teller. 'I have a joint account with my husband but I'm not sure if I have access to it—I think I signed the full authority over to him to manage the funds a few years ago. He told me it would be easier for him to manage the account that way,' I explained, 'because he would be needing to withdraw funds and manage the building project without having to get my permission for every withdrawal.'

The bank teller looked up my details. 'It looks like you actually have three authorities on that account,' she said. That's when I had a vague recollection of a meeting at the bank years earlier. The three signatories were my husband, my father-in-law and myself. I had mistakenly thought I had signed my authority away; now I realised that what had actually occurred, was that we had added my father-in-law onto the account as well. So, I had authority to access the account!

That was my first big moment of relief, but still I was unsure of what might come next. 'I'm not too sure how a joint account works,' I said. 'Can you tell me if I need joint permission to make a withdrawal?' 'No,' the teller replied, 'your name is on that account, so you can do whatever you like.' 'Well, I'm going to be managing some of the funds myself from here on, so can you tell me what happens if I want to move large quantities around, or make larger withdrawals?' I asked the question tentatively, hoping I wouldn't spark suspicion despite the fact I was still shaking a little. 'Do I need to get joint permission if the sum is over a certain amount?' 'No,' she simply said. 'Okay,' I clarified, 'so I can come in here and transfer money over from my joint account into my personal account at any time?' 'Yes, of course!' she replied. I thanked the teller, turned around, and walked out of the bank in disbelief. I had just managed to unlock a major amount of my finances that I thought I would never be able to access without my husband's help.

I went home and shared with a friend what had just happened. I told her how on moving day I would have to go to the bank and complete the transaction, and that this was going to add a lot of stress to what was already going to be a very full-on day for me. 'Why don't you just use internet banking?' she asked. 'Because I don't have access to those accounts on my internet banking,' I explained. 'I only have access to my personal account.' 'Well, you should be able to access them if you have a joint account,' my friend suggested. 'Why don't you ring the internet banking helpline?'

And so I made the call. 'Can you please arrange for all my accounts to show on my internet banking?' I asked, '. . . including my joint accounts?' The man on the other end of the phone pulled up our accounts on his screen. 'Well, that's strange,' he said, 'they should already be showing up. Let me look into it for a moment.' Soon he was back on the line. 'There's been a block placed here so that you cannot access your joint account via internet banking,' the man explained. 'Would you like me to reverse that for you?' 'Yes please,' I replied, and just like that, all the funds showed up on my screen! Now I was able to have full electronic access, so that on moving day, the transfer could be done at the click of a button before I left home. I could not believe it.

The next financial hurdle I faced was the need to access our 'working for families tax credit,' a lump sum which was given each year from the government for the purpose of assisting families with any needs they might have. It had always been very helpful for all the 'extras' such as school camps, uniforms and school fees, and I was not prepared to leave without it. The way my husband and I had set up his business, however, was with me as a shareholder. This meant that we both needed to fill out the forms required to get our family tax credit.

As I look back on the timeline of events, I can see that within a week of praying for clarity, I had received a book to listen to, a conference to attend, and a dream to orientate me. The following week I had written out out 'the plan' stipulating exactly what I needed in order to move out. The day after that, I received a vision about the bank and was able to secure my finances. And it was the very next day, following my visit to the bank, that I received a form in the mail for our 'working for families' tax credit! I remember thinking, 'Wow, this is moving fast. Two massive hurdles have been sorted for me in less than two days.' That very day, my husband and I sat down together, filled out the forms, and sent them off again. Neither of us enjoyed filling out forms but I remained firm with my resolve to get it done as quickly as possible and we tackled it together.

Getting my money from the bank and being able to receive our family tax credits had been non-negotiable in my mind; I was not prepared to leave with three kids while I was feeling financially vulnerable. Now, the financial door had swung open, leaving me with such a sense of relief and amazement at how quickly those matters had been resolved.

✓   The first trapdoor had been opened

Trapdoor 2: A Place to Live

The next issue I was unsure about was where we would go once we left. All I knew was that I needed a place that would feel safe and peaceful for myself and the kids. I thought about moving and all the 'stuff' we had accumulated over the years—having lived in a spacious house, one thing was sure, I would need to have a major sort-out. When I had first agreed that our 'safe exit' needed to be done quietly, without my husband knowing, I knew it would be a real feat to pull off unless I simply wanted to leave in the middle of the night with just a few suitcases. Now, I was facing the reality of what was involved.

'Lord,' I said once again. 'How am I going to navigate moving all our furniture and packing beforehand? I do not want to lie about anything at all during this process, so please, help me be honorable in how I go about this.' *I have put my words in your mouth,* he kept reminding me, and sure enough, the Lord kept inspiring me, dropping into my mind exactly what to say at each and every turn.

One day I came home and said to my husband, 'I've just had a great counselling session and I've decided to grow up and take responsibility for myself. I'm going to get fit and learn about running the business, and I'm also going to declutter the house and get rid of all the things that are causing stress in my life!' All of this was true and very heartfelt. I knew I needed to be in a healthy state of mind for leaving, and exercise would be a real help. I did want to understand how the business ran and knew I would need to know these details when I left. The decluttering was also on my radar as something I had wanted to do for a long time. If I decluttered, I was, in effect, getting ready so that we could take just what we needed with us on moving day. My husband's response was positive; he thought it all sounded like a very good idea. I too, was pleased with how it had come out. I had just given myself permission to prepare to leave—all out in the open.

Still, we would soon be needing accommodation. 'Lord,' I said, 'we've sorted the finances, but the next big thing is accommodation. What should I do?' In that moment, I felt the Lord answer me clearly and specifically: 'There's a cottage for you in Swanson.'

'Wow,' I thought. 'That sounds lovely.' I even felt a pang of excitement. I had always loved quaint cottages, and the thought of simplifying and going back to basics felt like such a weight off my mind.

As soon as I could, I searched online for houses to rent. Right away, a very quaint, cute and affordable cottage popped up—in Swanson! As I looked at the description and the pictures, it felt as if the home for rent was somehow a little part of 'me.' I soon realised, however, that I was nowhere near being ready to move. I hadn't begun packing, or even sorting through all our things. As I talked to the Lord about it, I said, 'Lord, it's really lovely but I'm just not ready. I'm going to trust instead that you will have the right cottage for me when I am realistically ready to move.'

Having gained momentum from seeing the financial trap doors open, energy seemed to come to me from out of nowhere. Until this time, I was predominantly glued to the couch, completely drained. Now, I took to the task of decluttering with gusto, moving quickly from room to room. Every day I would visit the fruit and vegetable shop, collect as many boxes as I could, and fill them up with the household items I no longer wanted. At the end of the day I would drive down to the local Salvation Army shop and donate all my goods. I was flying through it. At the same time, I took every opportunity to sit with my husband, diligently taking notes as he showed me the 'ropes' of our business—and, I began using our exercycle as much as possible. I was getting ready.

Two weeks later, I looked at my 'to do' list and thought, 'Wow, I'm really flying through this. I think I might even be ready to start looking for accommodation soon.' So once again, I sat down at the computer to browse through the available rental properties, only to find that the little cottage in Swanson was still on the website!

Swanson is a quaint little village and a much sought-after a place to live. It has a few local shops including a dairy that sells lovely fresh flowers, a hairdresser, chemist, cafes and an all-important local liquor store. I do love a good Merlot after all! Right across the road from the cottage was also a train station, which meant my son could easily get transport when he started his tertiary education the following year. He could roll out of bed literally one minute before the train left, and still make it on time—not that I would be encouraging that! My youngest who enjoyed scootering could spend hours at the skate park which was also directly across from the house. In every way, it seemed perfect.

That day, I called the agent and asked if the place was still available, or perhaps they had just forgotten to take it off the website? When she told me it was still available, I wondered why. Properties at the time were in hot demand and therefore hard to come by, especially if they had a bit of character. In fact, it was unusual in that market for a listing to last even a week, yet this cottage had been vacant for over a month.

'Oh,' I said, 'how come it has not been snapped up by now?' 'The landlord just hasn't found a suitable tenant yet' she replied—and in that moment, I knew that God had put that place on hold for me. The landlord hadn't found a suitable tenant *because I was the suitable tenant!* 'Great' I said, 'I'd like to come and see it.' 'Well, it's not that easy,' said the real estate agent, 'we don't just show anybody that's interested; if you want to take a look, you'll have to fill out some forms and we'll need to check out your references first.' And so, I got busy. Pulling everything together, I handed in my paperwork just a couple of days later.

Shortly after, the agent called, inviting me to view the cottage. What a lovely place. It had a warm, open-plan lounge, nice wooden floors in the kitchen and dining room, and, as females often do, I began to mentally dress the rooms with my furniture. The cottage had considerably less space than I was used to—the boys would need to somehow fit comfortably into one room, which concerned me a little—but I decided that the Lord had set this place aside for me and he would help me work out the details.

Once we'd looked around, the agent stood in the lounge area with me and said, 'I actually have ten people waiting in line for this property, and another person called me on my way here telling me that they would be happy to take the place right away, but your references were so good that you are our preferred tenant and we'd be happy for you to take it if you want it. You'll need to give me an answer straight away, though. Otherwise, I will pass the property on to the next person in line.'

This was the first time I had to make a concrete step forward, a commitment that would mean I would really go ahead with the decision to move out. I felt the weight of it in the moment, and in many ways it seemed so surreal, almost like a dream. I couldn't believe I was going to do this. 'I'll take it,' I said, and just like that it was actually happening. I came home with my head reeling from what had just happened and got in touch with my friend. 'The agent wants me to give her a move-in date,' I told her, 'and it has to be within the next two or three weeks.'

Now I needed to choose a date. If we were to achieve the 'safe exit' we were aiming for, I would have to pull off the move while everyone was out of the house. *What day, Lord?* I asked. 'How can I manage to get my husband and my kids out of the house for a full day?' It was the same question I had asked before: 'How do you want me to navigate this, Lord?'

A few days later, my friend and her husband came over to spend the evening at our place. For a few minutes, my friend and I talked together in my bedroom about the need to settle on a moving date, and before we went back upstairs to join the men, we simply prayed, leaving it up to the one who knows best. Later that night, a text came through to both our husbands' phones—it was an invitation to join a group of men who were going tramping on the third of June. I looked at the calendar. The third of June? That was in two weeks' time—on a Saturday! My husband had been on tramps with these friends before, and usually preferred to be dropped off at our church. From there, all the men would leave together and then be picked up again at the end of the day. 'What time will you need to be there?' I asked. 'Early,' he replied. 'Six-thirty a.m.' I shot a glance across to my friend. 'And what time will you be back?' 'Late. Eight-thirty p.m., they're saying.' 'Oh, okay,' I casually replied, but inside I was praying in astonishment, 'Thank you, Lord. You have set my moving-out date.'

Now I only had to work out what would happen with the kids. 'How am I going to see that they are also out for that day?' I asked my friend. 'Well,' she said, 'did you realise that's Easter weekend?' 'Oh,' I said, 'my son is already booked to go away on Easter camp for that whole weekend! I just need to find a few other places for the other two to go. Maybe they can stay at their friends' houses over that weekend and then we're sorted. That way I can set up the new place and get it ready for them to move into before they get back.'

The last thing I needed to do was to call the agent. 'There's only one date that works for me,' I said. 'Can we make it the third of June?' And with that, the date was set.

✓ Another trap door widely opened.

Trapdoor 3: Moving Date

That night, my husband and his friend began discussing how the group would get from the church to the start of the tramp. 'I could bring our eight-seater,' I heard him offer, 'so we can all travel together.' I froze for a moment. Normally, my husband drove his Land Cruiser, leaving me with the larger vehicle. 'I don't really want you taking the car that day,' I spoke up. He looked surprised at my emphatic reply. 'What do you need it for?' he asked. 'I might just need it,' I replied, and, seeing the puzzled look on my husband's face, we dropped the conversation. We were at a stalemate.

That night when I went to bed, I prayed again. 'Lord, how am I going to navigate the car situation? I don't want to lie, so please tell me—what should I do?' Right away, I felt the Lord say, 'Tell him you are helping a friend in a crisis situation on that day.' 'A friend, Lord?' I asked. 'Yes! Now, be a friend to yourself. Ask yourself for permission to help.' I sat there in bed feeling a bit strange about it all, but eventually said to myself, 'Cindy, will you help me move on Saturday with the car and trailer?' 'Yes, I will,' I said back to myself. 'There!' God said.

As we sat in the spa pool that week I brought up the subject once again. 'The real reason I need the car on Saturday,' I told my husband, 'is that I have agreed to help a friend who is in crisis that day, and I need the car and trailer.' My husband looked surprised and asked, 'Who is it?' 'I can't say,' I replied. 'She wants me to keep it confidential until after the move—then I'll be able to tell you.' 'Okay,' he said, and with that, the matter was settled.

✓   Another trapdoor passed through.

Trapdoor 4: Legal Rights and Bank Accounts

At that point I began to wonder what I was legally allowed to take with me when I left, and so, I made a call to my lawyer-friend. 'As their primary carer it is within your rights to take anything you need to provide for your kids,' I was advised. 'You can also take anything that you inherited as a gift.' With that in mind, I began walking around the house, making mental notes about what I would take.

During this time, I also received a verse from the Lord. It was Matthew 10:16 *Be wise as serpents and harmless as doves.* As I meditated on this scripture it became very important that I should not do anything out of malice, but only what was fair. As I made the decision about what to take with me and what should stay, I paid attention to Jimmy's 'favorite things'—a lounge suite and floor rug, a desk and dining table, our family computer . . . on the other side of the list were the things that had been given to me— my mother's grand piano, my nana's piano, and my grandfather's bookshelf. It felt good to 'get it right,' and if in doubt, to err on the side of leaving it for my husband.

I had told my husband, as he watched me declutter our home, that I was getting rid of every stress in my life. Now, I turned my attention to the digital side of things. The first thing I would need to do was to set up my own email account, rather than continue to use the address my husband and I had been sharing.

A year earlier, I had started the job of backing up our family photos; at this point I determined to finish the job, copying all our family movies and most precious memories onto USB sticks. I also told my husband that I wanted to declutter our inbox, where we had ten thousand emails banked up! I asked him to show me which emails were important to him, and sorted them into folders. I then sought the help of a computer savvy person from the kids' high school, who helped me set up an email account for my husband and showed me how to transfer all his important emails into his new account, ready for moving day, when I would shut down our joint account.

That week I also set up a post office box in Swanson, so that any mail that was related to the move, could be sent privately to me. From that point on, I organised everything on my smartphone, often when I was running errands or alone at home, being careful to do nothing on the family computer that could be traced.

Some moments, however, were touch and go. Although I had arranged for our utilities company to connect my phone to my new number on moving day, for some reason, they ended up turning off the power off at our home instead—a week before we were meant to leave! I found out when my husband found the power disconnected and had tried to call the telephone company to ask them what was going on. When he told me what he had done, my heart began racing and thumping in my chest. 'Oh no,' I thought, 'he's found out. They've told him there's been an arrangement to switch the power over to the Swanson address and I'm doomed!' However, he went on to say that when he tried to follow it up it sounded like a wrong number, and so he hung up.

'It must have been a mistake,' I said as casually as I could despite my pounding chest. Suddenly the stress of it all felt overwhelming; I felt weak all over, knowing it had been a close call. 'Don't worry about it,' I said. 'I'll call them back and sort it out. They've probably just made a mistake,' (which they clearly had). 'Besides,' I went on, 'the account is in my name, so they probably won't let you talk to them anyway.' Again, I was reminded of the verse, 'I have put my words in your mouth.' 'Thank you, Lord,' I breathed.

As soon as I could, I called the utilities company and had the power reconnected. I also told the operator that it was very important that this mistake should not happen again, and made sure that it was on their records that I was the only person who had authority to speak to them about the phone account. When I explained my situation, they apologised, and assured me it would not happen again.

I couldn't believe it, when, two days later the same thing happened! Now we had no internet *and* no phone. Once again, I put in a desperate call to the phone company asking them to put things right, only, it happened a third time as well! Now I was exasperated—and stressed to the max, especially when the support team from the telephone company called back right when I was standing in front of my husband and began asking me questions about my new address. Clearly, I was not able to answer the questions in front of him, and so I stood up, grabbed a box, and walked up into the attic to do some packing while talking to the phone support person, all the while hoping I was out of earshot of my husband. My husband, however, was curious to hear what the phone company had to say for themselves after such a major muck up third time round, and when I turned around, there he was, following me. Anxiously, I turned to him and said, 'I'm sorting it out! You don't need to follow me around!'

By now, I was rattled, and on edge. This time, I picked up another box and went down to the ground floor of the barn where I managed to find some privacy to finish the phone conversation and settle the debacle once and for all. I had always been so careful to do things in private. I did realise, however, after three incidents in a row with the phone company, that the enemy was trying to mess with 'the plan'—but that God had the master plan. Even though the situation seemed intense and I felt stressed, underneath it all, at a deeper level, I still had peace, a sense of knowing that God had my back and that he was in control.

✓   Another trapdoor navigated

Trapdoor 5: Income

Although my savings were secure, I did not want to use those funds for my weekly living costs. I had it on my heart to give the kids an inheritance and to make sure they were properly cared for well into their future. I left this with the Lord to sort out.

I also knew that I wasn't well enough to work at this stage, but still, I needed a regular income to support our family. I was grateful for the social welfare system of New Zealand and that I was able to secure a sickness benefit, amongst other allowances, that would enable me to move out and support my family. I know that some people feel embarrassed or humiliated by the thought of receiving that benefit. I, however, felt incredibly grateful, and knew it was only for a time until my health stabilised again. In the end, I understood that the system was set up for people in situations they might not have foreseen, and that, having paid taxes all of our working lives, it was perfectly reasonable to accept the help that was on offer now that we needed it. What I didn't know, was how much I might expect to receive.

As I sat opposite my case worker, waiting as she did the calculations, I held my breath, knowing that I had just committed to renting a house. I was trusting the Lord at every turn, and yet I felt like I was at their mercy. I needed to trust that there would be enough for me. When the case worker finally showed me the figure I would receive each week, I exhaled with relief and was reminded of the words, *My God shall supply all my needs.* 'You've got this God,' I thought—and it was true. With the amount available, I would be able to provide for the needs of my kids.

I came home that afternoon and mentioned to my husband that I had just been to the 'Work and Income' office to see if I could get extra financial support for the family. Somehow, through it all, I was able to remain as open and honest as I could be. I told him how I found out I was eligible for a counselling allowance and some support for medical expenses. This was all true. With my ongoing income now secured, I was set.

✓   Another trap door successfully passed through.

Trapdoor 6: Space for the kids

By now, I was noticing that the Lord would prompt me about who it was safe to share my plans with, and who it was best not to tell. The next day, I caught up with a close friend, someone I knew I could confide in. 'I am concerned about how small the bedroom is that my boys will have to share,' I mentioned. 'I'm not sure if both their beds can even fit into that space.' My friend immediately came back with a reply. 'What you need is a caravan,' she said. She went on to explain, 'Your son is eighteen. He'll think it's cool to have his own space. It will be like a teenagers' pad, a place for him to hang out in.' 'Perfect!' I said, and then prayed, 'Lord, where can I get a caravan from?' Instantly, another friend's name came to mind, and without sharing any details, I simply asked if she had a caravan or knew of anyone who had one. That friend gave me another woman's name, someone I had met once at a dinner.

When I called that number and began to speak, I felt confident about telling her my situation and asked her to keep it confidential. 'I'm looking for a caravan,' I said. 'I'm wondering if you might have one that you use for holidays that we could borrow for the rest of the year, perhaps?' 'I can do better than that,' she said. 'We actually have two caravans; one we use for holidays and one that just sits on our front lawn that the kids very rarely use. Every now and then they go there to hang out or play their guitars in it, but that's all. You can have it—use it for as long as you need it, free of charge, no worries at all! We're happy to help,' she assured me, 'and,' she said, 'I'm sorry to hear about your situation. If there's anything else we can do, just ask.'

I exhaled as a feeling of deep relief and excitement came upon me all at once. God had come through again. Wow. To see him work out every detail for me was a marvel. *'If there's anything else we can do, just ask!'* I thought for a minute and then replied, 'Well actually,' I said, 'on moving day it's going to be rather hectic and I may not have the time to come and collect the caravan from you. Would you mind dropping it off to my new place if I gave you the address? I can't promise to be there as I may still be shifting things back at the old place, but if you wouldn't mind backing it in and leaving it under the carport, I would be so grateful.' Her response was overwhelmingly accommodating—this family could not do enough for us. 'Not a problem,' she said, 'we'd be happy to help.' I told her how grateful I was, and said I would come over and thank her over a cup of tea or coffee once things had settled down. Then we said goodbye and ended the call.

As I sat on the side of my bed I had the strongest sense that I was getting caught up in what seemed like a surge, a rush of water that was moving forward whether I liked it or not; God had set something in motion, and nothing was going to stop it from happening. Things were falling into place rapidly, one thing after another. 'God,' I thought, smiling, 'you are simply amazing! It's true, isn't it? You will supply *all* my needs, according to your riches in glory.'

✓   Another trap door opened.

Trapdoor 7: Car Ownership

As a married couple, my husband and I jointly shared ownership of all our assets. Now, I turned my thoughts to our cars. The car I was driving was a large Toyota Prado, and I wanted to make sure I had the freedom to sell it and downsise my vehicle after I left. I had heard stories of people whose partners had turned up and legally taken their vehicles, using their spare key, because the ownership papers were in their name. Of course, the value of the cars would be halved for both of us eventually, but for now I needed to have the ownership papers transferred over into my name.

'I want to change the car ownership over into my name,' I said to my husband one day. 'Why?' he replied. 'Because you said that you want me to take full responsibility for the car, including any repairs and bills to do with the Prado, so it makes sense to change the ownership over.' 'There's no point,' he said, 'when I get the registration fee in the mail, I'll just hand it over to you.' 'No,' I said, 'I'd prefer to have it in my name; anyway, it only costs nine dollars to get it changed over, so I've decided I'm going to do that.' My husband just glanced over his shoulder and shrugged as if to say, 'if you want to, I guess.'

The next car to get changed over was my son's; it was also in my husband's name, which helped to bring the cost of insurance down. Now, however, it was important that my son had full control over his vehicle in case 'ownership' became an issue. As it so happened, my son had just finished paying off the small amount we had loaned him to help him purchase his first car, his pride and joy. That made it easier—I mentioned to my husband that our son had finally paid his car off and wanted to now get the car ownership transferred into his name. All I needed was his driver's license in order to fill out the forms. Right then, he handed his license to me, and I went into the bedroom, set out both the forms before me, and changed my son's car and mine, into our own names.

✓   Another trap door through

Trapdoor 8: Our Livestock

Our home was on a lifestyle block, where we had two sheep, five chickens and a large farm-dog called 'Friday.' How would I manage to rehome the animals in less than a week? 'Oh, Lord,' I prayed. 'What do I do? Wouldn't it look strange and a bit suspicious if all our animals suddenly disappeared?'

That week, one of our volunteer-workers came to us and told us that the sheep had started doing something strange—they had begun to randomly strip and eat the bark from our fruit trees! If the sheep kept it up, the volunteer said, the trees would soon die. We needed to do something about it—and fast! I told my husband that this was an urgent matter, that the workers were very concerned about the trees. Now we had a legitimate reason to have the sheep removed. These two sheep, affectionately known as Bobby and Splotch, were kindly on loan to us to help keep the grass down in the orchard; in turn, we helped by fattening up the sheep for their owners. It was a win-win situation . . . up until now. I called the owner and, after telling him that unfortunately, we would need to return his sheep, we wrestled and wrangled the overfed animals onto a caged trailer and returned them back to their happy homes.

Next, I turned my attention to the chickens, who, conveniently, had not been laying for a while. I had begun buying eggs from the supermarket, while still paying for feed for these rather beautiful but altogether unprofitable chooks of mine. Explaining my logic to my husband, I told him I was planning to put them up for sale. Someone would buy them for meat, no doubt, and my husband seemed pleased that I was making a sound financial decision. If the chooks were costing us money, they had to go. Later that week they were sold and carted off.

Friday, our family dog, was another matter entirely. She was a black collie crossed with a long-haired retriever that we had rescued when she was only six months old. Friday was an energetic puppy when she came to us—naughty, and incredibly difficult to retrain—but we loved her to bits. From day one, she stuck to us like glue and loved all the comings and goings at our place where there were people galore to bound around.

I had been told that we could have her at the cottage, but that she would need to be an outside dog only. The yard we were going to was so tiny, however, that it felt cruel to take her with us. Calling my friend who was a dog groomer and dog lover, I told her my dilemma. 'Have you thought about that couple up the road?' she asked. 'They're moving to Australia in a year's time, and I know they really want a family dog but can't commit to owning one long-term, but they might be interested in having her in the meantime. It would give them a great chance to experience having a dog.'

When I was able to catch up with the couple my friend had mentioned, I explained that our dog was becoming a bit of a nuisance for my husband (which was entirely true) and that he needed a break from her for a while (also true!). Would they mind having her, at least until they were ready to move? 'Yes!,' they replied, and a few days later, Friday went to stay with them, my husband was pleased with the newfound peace around our place, and though I was not ready to let her go completely, this felt like the perfect solution. For now, I could still visit her and take her for walks to the beach, all the while knowing that our much-loved dog had been welcomed into the home and hearts of a happy family.

✓   All the animals taken care of—in less than a week.

Trapdoor 9: Bits and Bobs

I was flying through my list and had come to the home stretch. Now there were only the remaining loose ends that needed tying up. Selling things online had certainly made a difference as we got rid of items like the deep freezer and a table tennis table—things we no longer needed or used.

With one more week before moving day, it was time to think about picking up a few appliances and furnishings for our new house. I needed a refrigerator and a dining room table to start with, and soon found what I was looking for—a small but extendable dining-room table was listed for just ninety-five dollars, which I quickly purchased. With its quaint legs and lovely wooden finish, I could see it fitting perfectly in our wee cottage, and arranged for my friend to pick it up and deliver it so I would not need to store anything at our home prior to the big move. Online, I also found a cheap fridge with the perfect dimensions to fit the space in the kitchen. Because my husband and I had a shared trading account, I asked a friend to bid for it on my behalf and arranged other friends to collect and deliver that item on moving day.

As part of my plan to leave well and take what I needed, I remembered a few other things that were important to me. My dad had gifted me some lovely Rimu wood from an old house he had lived in that ended up being demolished. Eventually, I thought, a dining room table made from that would be a really nice idea. That week, I asked a friend if he would take the wood and store it for me until I could put it to use.

Leaving no stone unturned, I even decided I would like to have a trailer-load of mulch delivered to my new place so I would have it there, ready for when I would be ready to plant a new cottage garden. Though I wasn't sure if we would have time for this on moving day, I had a friend with their trailer ready to go on stand-by, just in case.

✓   Another trap door opened

Trapdoor 10: My Baby Grand Piano

By now, as the Lord continued to prompt me, I had begun letting some of my friends know about my plans to move out—and everyone wanted to help on moving day. To make the most of their generous offers, I prepared a sheet of information, including an inventory of each room, a diagram of my new home along with details of the new address and directions about where to find the house key, and instructions showing which room each box needed to go into.

There turned out to be ten helpers—exactly one person for each space that needed to be packed and moved, and those who could fit boxes into their cars were more than happy to help me at the other end as well. One dear friend said he wanted to give me four hundred dollars towards my moving costs, since he couldn't be there in person on the day. He also told me he would like to help me out with the bond, knowing I would not be able to access my funds beforehand. That same friend also booked and paid a deposit on a moving truck for the third of June. What a gift!

Now I had just one more concern—what to do with my baby grand piano. There was no way it was going to fit into my snug little cottage. It needed to go someplace else. The piano came as an inheritance from my mother, but to understand just how much that piano meant to me, we need to go back in time . . .

I learned to play the piano from a very young age. I loved the sound of the instrument; its tone and richness of sound moved my spirit every time I heard it being played. As a teenager, I played this beautiful instrument for hours on end, getting swept up as I sang and played worship songs and often, writing my own songs. My brothers seemed to loathe waking up at six-thirty a.m. to the sound as I practiced my scales in preparation for my piano exams. For me, though, it was a pure joy and delight. It was part of me.

My husband's head injury soon after we were married left him unable to tolerate noise or movement—suddenly, I was unable to play the piano in my own home! And so, having no choice but to accept it, I closed that chapter of my life and moved on . . . or so I thought. After we moved into 'the barn-house,' however, I began to notice that I became deeply moved whenever I heard the sound of a piano being played, whether I was out and about or simply listening to a recording. It moved me to tears. 'Lord, why are you doing this to me?' I asked many times. 'You know I can't have a piano in the home because of my husband's needs; why, then, are you stirring up so much emotion in me?' Deep down I knew that the Lord was using the power of that emotional response to ask me what I really wanted. But the question was too hard to answer. 'Don't make me say it, Lord,' I replied. 'Arghh!' I was feeling so upset and angry.

Eventually, in a frustrated outburst, I gave him my reply. 'You know what I want, Lord! I just want to be able to play the piano in worship for you. There! Are you happy?! I said it!' At that time, I had been looking after my nana's upright piano, which was tucked away on a concrete floor downstairs in the barn. What

I really wanted, though, was to be able to play *upstairs*, where it was light and where I could enjoy playing it. 'You really shouldn't have asked me, Lord,' I went on, 'it's just cruel, because you know I'm not able to do that.'

It was just a week after my moment of prayerful angst, that my mum called me to tell me she wanted to gift me her baby grand piano. I was the one who learned to play it, she explained, and since there was no longer any space to store it at her place, she decided that I should rightfully have it. We both cried—my mum was the one who best remembered how much my music had meant to me; she knew my situation and understood the loss I felt. 'I know, Cindy,' she said. 'I understand. I only felt it right to ask you anyway.' 'Mum,' I said, 'I can only ask. I'll get back to you soon.' I went to my husband and simply set my request before him. 'I've inherited my mother's baby grand piano,' I said, 'and I would like to bring it home and keep it upstairs. Can I do that?'

There was no coercion at my end. I just needed to ask, though I didn't hold much hope. Many times I had asked my husband if we could bring my nana's piano upstairs and every time I had been refused. But this time, my husband surprised me. After just a short pause, he looked at me and said, 'we'll make it work.' I couldn't believe it, in fact, I was stunned. Promptly, I called my mother and said, 'Quickly! Get it over here before he changes his mind!'

So, that is how the baby grand came into my home. Though I had not asked for it, the Lord had other plans. Where there had been a drought for so many years, I now felt his desire to lavish his gifts on me and give back in abundance what had been lost.

I tried to play the piano when my husband was out of the house, and although I was very rusty, it didn't matter—I was beginning to play again, and the tears of healing flowed freely as I tuned into the deep longings within me just to sing and play once again. And so, the baby grand was not just a 'nice' piano to me—it symbolised so much more than that.

Now, as I faced moving on, the thought that I might not be able to take my piano with me left me feeling a little numb. I had resigned myself to the possibility that I was going to have to leave it behind and hopefully, if things were amicable enough between us after the move, I could sort it out at a later date. That same day, however, my doctor, who was a Christian and knew I was leaving, turned to me in the middle of my appointment and asked, quite randomly, 'What about your piano?' Startled by her question, I simply looked at her, but she carried on. 'You need to get it out of the house. If he sees the piano as some kind of extension of you, he might take to it with an axe.'

This was confirmation that the Lord wanted me to take it with me, but 'where Lord? I prayed. 'I have no clue. Who on earth is going to have room to store a grand piano?' My doctor made some enquiries with her musical friends, but to no avail. Nevertheless, I added it to the end of my list of final things to tend to before the move. In reality, though, I was stuck—and I only had five days to go.

In the end, I decided to go ahead in faith and book a moving truck for the piano. Knowing it was a specialist job, I called a piano moving company to ask for a quote. 'Where is the piano to be picked up from?' they asked. I gave them our barn address. 'And where is it to be delivered to?' I paused. 'Well, I don't actually have an address for you just yet, but I will have one by moving day. If I just give you my cottage address for now, can you give me a quote?' 'Certainly' the man replied, 'that will come to four hundred dollars.' At the mention of that amount, I suddenly remembered the money that my friend had gifted me towards the move—four hundred dollars exactly!

I sat in my car just days from the move with no place to move the piano to. 'Lord,' I said, 'how do you want me to navigate this one? I have run out of options. Tell me right now where the piano needs to go. It's the last thing I need to sort out on my 'to do' list, and I'm not leaving this car until I get an answer.' I sat there and waited. I wasn't praying, I was just simply waiting—impatiently, I might add. And then, just minutes later, the words, 'Excel School of Performing Arts' popped into my head. This was a Christian tertiary institute about twenty minutes' drive from where I lived. Picking up the phone, I called the number and spoke to the director, who was a stranger to me, but I asked if the school might enjoy using my grand piano until I resettled. 'It could take a couple of years,' I explained.

The director was concerned that the piano might be a bit too precious, and because he couldn't guarantee that it would be returned in pristine condition, he declined the offer. I hung up the phone and sighed as if to say, 'Yeah, okay, God. Now what's your big plan?' The problem was, as I sat there looking up at the sky, I couldn't seem to shake the word, 'Excel' from my mind—and so, I called the director back again. 'Look,' I said, 'I'm desperate. I have nowhere else to put this thing. I'm happy to accept that it may not be returned in pristine condition, but for now, it just needs a home.' By the end of the call, the director agreed. 'We will do our very best to take good care of it and to keep it covered whenever it's not in use,' he said. I exhaled with relief. The last major thing had just been taken care of, and with that, a deep peace began to settle over me.

✓　　　Final Trap Door opened

THE CONFERENCE

My desperate prayer for clarity led not only to the Lord giving me my vivid seven-part dream, but it had also brought two distinct directives from the Lord. Firstly, that I should listen to the audiobook that he had persistently brought to my attention; and secondly, that I was to attend the 'Women of Courage' conference I had heard advertised on our local Christian radio station. Knowing that he had some things he wanted to impart to me while I was there, and having just completed all my 'to do' list, my mind felt free. The organizational side of the move had all been arranged; now it was as if the Lord wanted to prepare me personally, to relieve me of the anxiety that often gripped me, filling me with adrenaline until I was almost constantly trembling. But I was ready and open to receive from the Lord all that he wanted to impart into my spirit.

The conference was held in the city of Hamilton, a few hours away from where I lived. I had arranged to stay with my aunty while I was there for the weekend, but felt strongly that I shouldn't share with her at this stage that I was moving out. My kids were at home that weekend, under the watchful eye of our boarder. Things were always better at home with a third party in the mix, and our boarder was an incredible blessing. Now I had the chance to catch up with my aunt—in many ways, I felt that we were kindred spirits. She too had been through some very tough times and had suffered enormous tragedy and trauma in her life. We had a lot in common. We both loved the Lord dearly and clung to him through all our valleys, and whenever we met together, we would share, pray and encourage one another. I thanked God in advance for the lovely weekend we were about to share, praised him for what he was going to do through the conference, and set out with great expectations that he was going to meet me there.

The speakers that year, as it turned out, were courageous Godly women who had left destructive or abusive marriages of their own, and not only survived, but thrived! In addition to the main sessions, there was also plenty of ministry time available, and whenever it was offered, I went forward, hungry to receive all that the Lord had in store for me. That weekend, the Lord did a deep work in me as I began to lay down all my fears. The fear of not being provided for, the fear of what people might think or say about my decision to leave . . . I laid it all down at his altar.

One of my cries was, 'God, I don't want to be stuck in a daily grind, just trying to provide for the kids and myself. My deepest desire is to be free to serve you, to write the book you've asked me to write and to speak to others about the things you have placed on my heart. That's my heart's desire, Lord. If you can take care of my finances, I will serve you with all that I have.'

At times during the conference there were scheduled breaks, where, more often than not, I retreated to my car because it felt like I was having a sacred moment with the Lord. It was as if he really wanted to speak to me—not only through the speakers and ministry team, but on my own. He was drawing me away, and I sought out privacy, a quiet place to meet with him, to ponder and reflect, and to listen to his voice.

It was during one of those breaks that I began thinking about what I should do with the savings that I had secured. I sat and pondered. What I really wanted to do was give an inheritance to each child to help with their first home. 'God,' I said. 'I want that money to stay safe and not be spent.' Right then, I remembered a conversation with my lawyer friend, and, though it was some time ago, his words came back to my mind: 'What you really need to do is to put your money into a trust.'

As a family, only a few weeks earlier, we had looked into setting up an account for our children through a Christian Trust fund[8]. It had seemed a solid way to invest, and operated on good biblical principles, and now, as I sat in the car, I brought the idea before the Lord once again. 'Lord, is that the right thing to do? Please give me wisdom,' I asked.

With the lunch break nearly over, I quickly finished my sandwich and returned to my seat, although my inner dialogue continued even as the speaker made his way to the platform. Little did I know how his words would speak straight into my heart! This man ran an orphanage for girls in India, and the very first thing he began to talk about, was how he felt that God had asked him to completely surrender his personal finances to him, and that as he did that, God drew him deeper and deeper unto him. I knew that this was the one area I had not fully surrendered to God, but as the speaker went on to say how he felt that God wanted him to give an inheritance to the girls under his care and that he was to put his personal money into investing into some land for the girls for their future homes, my spirit leapt. This was the perfect confirmation for what I was thinking. There I was, only minutes before, asking the Lord what I should do with my personal savings and whether it was right for me put it towards an inheritance

---

8 Liberty Trust, a NZ-based entity.

for the children for their first homes. 'Wow,' I thought. 'God answered me almost instantly! One thing's for sure—walking in faith is certainly not boring.'

The conference speaker conveyed how he wanted to tread lightly on the earth, knowing his true treasure lay in heaven. I was deeply moved at those words, and with full agreement in my spirit, I sensed God drawing me back to simplicity. I knew there was no doubt this was God confirming to me that yes, going ahead with a Trust for my children was the right thing to do.

The next speaker talked about how true tithing is about giving to widows and orphans, and how, when we align our finances rightly, everything else also falls into alignment—in our health, body, mind, spirit and soul. I had sometimes thought about the love of money being the root of all evil, but had not considered how it could affect our health in all these areas. It was time to fully surrender my finances to the Lord. As I sat there, the amount of money that I should set aside as an inheritance for the children came to mind, and when I worked out the remaining amount, it came to ten per cent! This would be my tithe! I had been wondering whether or not to keep the rest as a safety net, but after that session, I knew God what wanted me to do. With a joyful heart, I decided I would give ten per cent of my funds to an orphanage he had placed on my heart, and with that, a deep peace washed over me.

The conference was wonderful—a chance for just me and God, a time for him to speak to me, challenge me, and fill me up. On the last day, I felt him say, 'Today, I want you to just receive from me.' At every opportunity that day, I went forward for prayer ministry. I was expectant, and desperately hungry for him, and at one stage a woman prayed and began to laugh as the Holy

Spirit came upon us. After she prayed, I went away with such an excitement in my gut—it felt as if I were a little kid the night before Christmas—I couldn't stop grinning from ear to ear, and once again, a tremendous peace came over me.

I returned home from the conference full of joy and thanksgiving in my heart. I thought about the verse that the Lord had given me to meditate on throughout this journey: *The cowering prisoners will soon be set free!* Yes, it was nearly time. Every day leading up to the move, I began to play loud worship music as the words, 'you shall go out with joy and be led forth with peace,' rang in my heart. One song in particular was constantly on my lips: *Be still. Let your voice be all I hear now.* I knew that as long as I focused on the Lord, I would be okay, that fear would not creep in or cripple me. I had such peace! I tried to keep things as normal as possible at home so as not to raise suspicion. I also did not want to create any tension that might cause my husband to flare up again. The kids had been through enough, I decided, and I was not going to allow them to be subject to any more suffering. So, in the end, our home life in the week leading up to the move was strangely peaceful—almost surreal.

My eldest son left for camp on the Thursday night before Easter weekend, and when Friday came, I dropped my other two off at their friends' homes, gave them a kiss and waved goodbye. A twinge of sadness came over me, knowing that tomorrow their lives were about to change forever. I struggled with wanting to tell them before the move, wishing I could spare them the shock when they returned, but the thought of them having to go through the turmoil of not knowing how their father would react, along with the wisdom and professional advice I had sought, played over in my mind. 'Safety first,' I thought. 'Keep them physically and psychologically safe.' Still, I cried at the thought that they had just left behind forever, their lovely bedrooms, their family home, and a father whom they still loved, despite everything that had gone on. 'Lord, this is just so hard,' I began to weep.

SPEEDBUMP

It was now Friday, and our tradition every Friday night was for the family to watch a movie and grab some takeaway pizzas to eat together. Tonight, however, with the kids already gone for the weekend, it was just our boarder, my husband, and myself, at home. 'I'll pick up the takeaways,' my husband said later that evening, and reached for his set of keys. The problem was, a few days earlier, after taking over the ownership of the car, I had decided to take the spare key off my husband's keyring, thinking he wouldn't notice.

Now, he came storming towards me. 'Where's the key for your car?' he demanded. 'Why did you take the spare key off my key-ring?' I was frozen, lost for words. 'Lord,' I shot up a quick prayer, 'You said you would put the words in my mouth.' 'Well,' I said, 'I don't keep a spare key for your car, so why should you keep one for mine? Why don't you drive your own car down to the take-away shop? After all, you do have a car sitting down there that is yours.' My husband was furious. 'Fine,' I said, 'I'll go and get you your spare key.'

'Oh, Lord. How am I ever going to get that key back?' I wondered. Even though I had carried such peace, the adrenaline had started to kick in again. Tomorrow was moving day and I knew now that it was going to take everything out of me—physically, mentally and emotionally.

THE NIGHT BEFORE THE MOVE

My husband and I had been mostly sleeping in separate rooms and each bedroom door had a lock on it. I had thought at the time when we had built the house, that this was unnecessary and a bit of an overkill decision. By this time, however, the lock on my door had become a Godsend, giving me a safe place for planning, emailing and texting, and to generally make arrangements.

That night it was midnight by the time everyone had headed to their rooms and gone to sleep. Quietly, I went into the lounge and shut down all our joint accounts—TradeMe, YouTube, and our joint email address—and I cleared all the browsing history. I wanted a clean break. No more joint *anything*. At two a.m. I crawled back into bed. With a wake-up time of six-thirty, I knew I would be heading into a full-on day, with very little sleep behind me. 'Give me the rest I need, Lord,' I prayed.

MOVING DAY

6.15 a.m. I wake to my husband's early rise. He is getting picked up at 6.30 a.m. I can hear him having breakfast, and I feel the Lord's prompting, telling me to *go now* and get the spare car key off his keyring. I walk quietly down to the other end of the house. I check in his wardrobe where he normally keeps his keys and . . . it's not there! *Why would he have his keys with him if he is catching a ride with someone else?* I think. *They must be in the pocket of the pants he is wearing, or in his backpack.* Creeping out of the bedroom, I notice his bag sitting at the top of the stairs, ready to go. I feel the lid and hear the rustle of the keys. Quietly, I unzip the lid of the bag, gently pick up the keys, and try to pry the spare car key off. I can hear my husband washing his breakfast bowl and know he will be down here any second now. The keyring is stiff and the key won't come off. I start to panic. My hands are shaking like a leaf. I give it a good strong push and it comes loose, unthreading all the other keys off the keyring as well. Quickly, I slip the spare key into my dressing gown pocket, thread the other keys back on, and place the keyring back inside the backpack lid. I close the zip. Done. Phew! With my heart racing, I dart into the nearby bathroom and lock the door.

While I'm in the bathroom, my friend shoots me through a text to say her husband is running late. *No! Not today!* I think to myself. If my husband is ready and waiting, chances are he will go straight to the computer to check his emails or watch YouTube. Then he will notice that everything is shut down. I shoot a text back. 'Hurry! I've changed things in the night on the computer. If he gets on while he's waiting, I'm in trouble!' Now, I'm praying. 'Please, Lord, steer him away from the computer!' A few minutes later, I hear him walk past the bathroom and grab his backpack. I call out, 'Have a good tramp!' 'Okay,' he says. I watch him drive away. 'He's gone!' I think. 'It's all on now!'

Our home was a large barn with a workshop downstairs and seven big wooden barn doors that opened up onto our gravel driveway. Upstairs was our home. It was huge—five hundred square meters in total, and big sweeping rural views all around us. Seven bedrooms and a large open plan living area with two lounges, a very comfortable rustic kitchen and a spacious dining area meant that there was always room to fit plenty of people. Now, however, we needed to clear the place out.

Running downstairs, I flicked on all the inside and outside lights, as it was still dark outside, and flung the barn doors open, ready to receive the 'army' of friends who would soon be arriving. Then

I headed back upstairs and into the lounge where I flicked open our internet banking, pulled out my calculator, and began dividing everything in half, transferring the money, one account after another, into my personal account. Done! 'Breathe,' I told myself, ' . . . and eat some breakfast!' I sat down with my head in a spin, not knowing what to do next as I mechanically ate some muesli. By now, it was seven a.m. In half an hour, my friends would be arriving with boxes, tape and marker pens, ready to pull off our move. 'Time to wake my boarder and tell her the news.'

I knocked on her bedroom door. 'Can I come in?' I asked, 'there's something important I need to tell you. Do you trust me?' I had been mentoring this girl for more than a year by now, and we had built up a good bond between us. Still, she looked at me sleepy and bewildered. 'Yeah, sure. What's up? Are you okay?' 'Honey, I have to move out for the kids' safety, and it's happening right now while their dad is away on his tramp.' I started to cry. 'I'm really sorry I couldn't tell you sooner, but you need to pack up today and go back to your family.'

I knew that our boarder's family were keen to have her move back in with them whenever she wanted—they lived nearby and had kept her old bedroom waiting for when or if she ever decided to return. 'My friends are coming to help me move at seven-thirty,' I said, 'the moving truck will be here at nine, and I need the bed you are sleeping on. It belongs to my mum and I'm taking it with me. When things settle, I will come and visit and explain everything to you.' I gave her a big hug and with that she got up and began packing her things. I felt so bad.

My friends rallied as planned. Ten people for ten spaces in the house that needed packing out—I had not planned it that way, but the numbers were just perfect! *That's just like my Maker,'* I thought, '*He works every detail out.*'

I had asked my friends to bring enough boxes on packing day for the rooms they would be responsible for so we could avoid suspicion prior to the move. Now, everyone went to work quickly and diligently. There was a sense of urgency. The mood was somber, yet I felt a strong sense of togetherness. I was not alone; the Lord had provided me with the support, help and care that I needed for the day. With my inventory for the items that needed to be packed from each room, everything was running smoothly.

At nine a.m. the truck arrived with two men who began shifting the furniture and boxes into the truck. Thankfully, they were also able to fit my nana's upright piano into the truck. I was pleased. There would be music in my home!

Harry, my handy-man, had become like a father to me ever since my dad had passed away—and that day, he took me under his wing. He and another friend worked together, dismantling bed-heads, unhinging doors to help furniture slip through tight spots, and even carefully removing a wooden board that was nailed to the wall with all the kids' heights at different ages marked on it. Those two men also shoveled the mulch I had requested onto a trailer, carried boxes around for me, and even managed to collect the refrigerator I had bought from an online seller.

Next to arrive were the grand piano movers. They came in, took one look, and decided they would need to come back another day. 'The only way to get the piano out,' they said, 'is through the sliding door, down a makeshift ramp, and then to carry it down an uneven grassy slope. We could try bringing it through the house, but the piano will not fit around the corner of the stair-well.' While the men continued to assess the situation, rain had begun drizzling outside, only adding to the difficulty.

'No,' I insisted, 'it must be moved today.' A steely sort of resolve had set in; I knew that there had to be a solution. One of the piano movers called his boss and started walking towards me as he talked. 'Excuse me, Cindy,' he said. 'I'm really sorry, but because it's trickier than I thought, we have decided we can do it, but it will cost another eighty dollars.' The man looked apologetic as he waited for my reply. *Is that all?!* I thought to myself, knowing that there was no way to place a value on how important it was for me to see it moved out, safe and secure. 'That's fine,' I said. 'Just do whatever it takes to get the piano out today.' As I watched the baby grand being half slid, half pushed down the slippery slopes outside my lounge window I had another surreal moment. *Is this really happening?* I think I was in shock.

At times, that morning, I sat in the kitchen, stunned. A whirl of activity was happening around me, but friends gently came alongside, asked me if I was okay, and reminded me to eat. Still, I had moments where I came close to falling apart. In my son's room was a small rimu table that my husband had made for me while we were dating. A friend noticed that it wasn't on the inventory of things to take from that room and came to check with me about it. 'Do you want to take that small table?' she asked. 'No,' I said, but a pang of pain ran through me, and I began to cry, knowing it would hurt my husband to see it left there too, and in that moment, I knew how much I still cared for him.

With the house cleared out, we closed the doors for the last time and my crew of friends and I headed for the cottage. On the way, my girlfriends stopped to pick up fresh coffee orders for us all, and food to prop me up for the task that still lay ahead. It was a surreal moment as we drove from one house to the next. We had begun to pack, from scratch, that morning; suddenly, the entire moving-out process was over, and it was only one p.m.!

From there, many of my friends said goodbye for the day, and a smaller group of us began to unpack the furniture and boxes at the cottage. I appreciated the help with setting up the kids' beds and placing their clothes into drawers, but the rest I was happy to leave for later on that week. 'What a faithful group of friends I have,' I thought, as I looked around at everyone who had been so willing to help. It felt as if an army had marched in, picked me up, and carried me to out of there. Though I had just walked away from a lot of material things, I felt so rich—rich in community, rich with love, and rich with an exceptional God whom I could lean on and trust in for everything that I would need.

DISCLOSURE

I had worked out how I would tell my husband that I had moved out after discussing it in detail with several trusted friends and with professionals. 'Be wise as serpents and harmless as doves,' was the verse I continued to defer to. It was very important to me that I take as much care as possible to make sure he also would be safe and cared for after my departure. I had chosen not to tell any of his friends that I was planning on moving. If he thought they had known beforehand, I knew he might discard them as friends, just when he would need them most. I wanted to ensure that my husband would have a strong group of friends he could trust and confide in afterwards. I also wanted to make sure that his parents would be at the barn when he arrived home; I arranged for them to come over for dinner around the time that Jimmy would be arriving home, and I left a pot of soup on the stove for them. He would need their support.

Around six p.m., I got a call from my husband to say they had arrived back at the church, and could I come? I felt nervous and apprehensive as our friend, Harry, drove my husband's car to a nearby McDonalds carpark and left it there; from there, Harry, his wife and I went to pick up my husband who was cold and agitated because I was 'late.' I told him that we had been helping someone move all day, and then suggested, 'since Harry and his wife are still here with us, let's call into McDonalds for a quick cup of coffee our way home.' My husband was not impressed and said he just wanted to get home, but I brushed off his comments and said, 'it won't take long.'

We were waiting in the queue to buy our drinks, when my husband turned to me and said, 'look, I'm really cold and tired—if you want to stay here and have a drink, that's fine, but could you please just drop me off at home first?' He was agitated and I was nervous. 'We need to talk,' I said. 'It won't take long. I just need you to sit down here at this table for a minute.' My husband could sense the seriousness in my voice and tentatively sat down beside me with Harry and his wife on the other side of the table in case things got out of hand. Without any of us knowing how he might react, we had chosen to tell him in a public place, in the hopes of avoiding confrontation as much as possible.

I took a deep breath, 'Well,' I said, 'you know how I have been unhappy with the way you have been treating me and the kids, and it has become quite serious now for me. Some of the things you have done have been against the law, it is abuse, and I've decided that this will no longer continue. I have not decided at this stage whether or not I am going to press charges against you for what you have done.' My husband was nodding his head and seemed to be agreeing with me that it had to stop. He was taking it in. I took another deep breath. 'And for that reason, I have decided to move out—today.' Now my husband looked shocked. 'Everything I want to say to you is written in this letter,' I said as I handed him a large white envelope. 'It has some important information in there for you including things like your new email address, which you will need.'

I placed his car keys on top of the envelope and told him that his car was out in the carpark and that he could make his own way back to the barn. At that point, my husband stood up and simply said, 'Well, if I can get my backpack out of your car, I'll be on my way then.' Leaving the envelope behind on the table, he headed for the door. 'Take it to him,' I said to Harry. 'It's important, he needs it.' I had made a second copy, just in case, which I could give to his father to pass on to him at a later stage if need be. But Harry managed to get to the truck in time to place the envelope through the window, and onto the passenger seat before my husband charged out of the carpark.

I felt stunned, completely numb. In the space of about five minutes, it had all been over. I had been expecting an angry outburst, a fist fight, or some other volatile scenario, but now, he was simply and abruptly, gone, and though it was hard to watch, I knew that I had made the right decision.

It is never okay to allow your children to live in an abusive situation—God knows that, and I knew it too. It was also against the law for me, as their caregiver, to sit idly by and watch my children be mistreated and abused. There are laws to keep us safe and to give us order in the land, and I thank God for the law and for the justice system. Now, it was time to come under the protection of that law, for the sake of my children.

Make no mistake, however—I am pro-marriage all the way. But when this sort of behaviour is carrying on in front of your eyes, and your husband refuses to acknowledge that he is not treating the children right, or will not seek help and take responsibility for his own actions, then it is time to put a stop to it.

The letter I wrote to my husband affirmed him and honoured him in all the ways that he was good. I thanked him for the many good things he had done, but I also went on to explain that his behaviour was unacceptable, and how grieved I was that he had not accepted full responsibility for his actions and would not apologise or get help despite my asking.

My hope for the future was that my husband would have a restored relationship with the Lord and begin to restore his relationship with his children. I knew I had to keep the door of communication open for that to happen, but first I just needed time to recover. We all did, and so, the approach moving forward would have to be wise and considered—small doses of contact, with safety measures in place.

Unfortunately, by the time my husband arrived back at the barn, his parents had got tired of waiting, and had left. I wished we hadn't been running so late, and not everything had gone according to my plan, but I had done my best to make sure Jimmy was going to be okay. Now, I asked a friend to call his father and explain what had happened. I will never forget what my father-in-law said in reply: 'Tell Cindy we love her, and that we have observed that his behaviour towards her and the children has been appalling.' I needed to hear those words, to hear that it wasn't 'just me,' that I wasn't 'making it up' or going crazy. We really had been living in a terrible situation.

It took a while for my father-in-law to catch up with my husband; for a good few hours they seemed to miss each other, as both of them came and went from the barn. Eventually, however, they made contact. Knowing that, I felt relieved and settled. He now had the support of his family, and from this point on, he would also have the support of his friends. 'Be as gentle as a dove'—I reminded myself that I had done the best I could, and that he would continue his journey with his support network safely around him.

I came home that night to a home cooked meal that my friend had made for me—my favourite lasagna, and a good Merlot. My friend then stayed with me through the night so I would not be alone. The next morning, she waved goodbye, and just five minutes later, another friend turned up and together we began to unpack all my kitchen things. As I began to look around, it struck me that I had far too many cushions, and definitely too much artwork for my small new home. It was time to simplify. The next night, with everything culled and sorted, a deep peace washed over me and for the first time in many weeks, I slept soundly.

GENTLY GOES...

The next day was Monday, and with the kids returning home that afternoon, our friends, Harry and Mary, along with another couple, came around in the morning and worked on setting up the caravan for my son to move in to. It was winter, after all, and we needed to make sure he had adequate heating and lighting out there. With permission from the owners, they were able to reconfigure the lounge to fit his full-sized bed in sideways. It was a perfect fit—snug, but perfect.

Letting the children know what had happened was not going to be easy. I had spent a lot of time in prayer over this prior to the move and had discussed it with my friend who was a child psychologist. 'What is the best approach?' I asked. 'What is the least damaging way to go about doing this?' Realistically, it was never going to be easy. It would be hard, but I was encouraged to be gentle and to be careful not to overwhelm them with too much information at once. If I could deliver the news in a calm tone, it would help my kids feel that everything was going to be okay.

I had sought the Lord about how and where I should tell them. I couldn't take them back to the barn—that would be too shocking. I couldn't take them straight to the new home without first having explained everything—that would be equally shocking. I certainly did not want to tell them in any sort of public place. They needed to hear the news somewhere where it was safe for them to express their emotions.

As I prayed, the Lord had given me a vision of a loungeroom belonging to a friend of mine who was a widow and lived on her own. She would stay away for the afternoon, we agreed, at least until I had finished explaining what had happened to the kids. As it turned out, her home was the perfect place for us to meet— private, warm and 'neutral.'

I picked up the kids one by one and when all three were in the car, explained that we were going to head over to my friend's house to have a chat about dad and his head injury related behaviour. This was not particularly unusual—from time to time we would go away for a weekend just to get some respite, or to debrief about how they were finding things with dad and head-injury related behaviour. At other times we would just go out for milkshakes to chat about how they were doing with it all. And so, they took it in their stride when I said we were going to talk it through again, and not much else was said.

My friend had kindly left some food and drinks out for us on the coffee table, and as we sat down, my kids started hoeing into the food like typical teenagers. A few minutes later, I asked them how they were finding things with their dad. 'Not great,' they said. I then began to explain to them that his behaviour was, in fact, not acceptable, it was actually abuse, and gently I told them that the situation we had been living with was not okay, that they did not have to live like that anymore. 'On the weekend, I moved us out,' I said.

Each of the kids had different reactions, and we took our time to work it through as a family. My heart was so heavy. I wanted to wrap each one of them in cotton wool and protect them from any more harm. *They've been through enough Lord,* I whispered, *please take care of them.*

An hour or so later, I brought them back to their new home and they unpacked their belongings quietly. I had asked the Lord to help prepare their hearts as much as possible and in many ways he had opened their eyes and given them an understanding that things were not okay during the weeks leading up to the move. They had begun sharing things with me—new insights—and I knew that God had already been answering my prayers and preparing their hearts.

In the weeks that followed, the love I received from my community was overwhelming. People brought meals and baking to our home. A close friend flew up from another city to be with me. Someone else gifted me with a computer, since I had left the family one behind. As friends came and went, I thought, 'This is what church looks like. I am rich in community, I am loved, and that is enough for me.'

RESTORING RELATIONSHIPS

A number of issues had been clamoring for my attention, until they got to the point where I could ignore them no longer. The most important, of course, were to do with custody for our children and how the property would be settled. Now, I knew it had to be done; the trouble was, I simply did not have the capacity to work through these issues. With the physical move behind me, I was completely spent. It had taken all of my energy to get to this point, and now I had collapsed. I needed someone to be my spokesperson, someone fair and good at mediating who would be my advocate.

Several names ran through my mind but I kept coming back to my brother. Things had been strained between us for several years and I was nervous about the thought of approaching him to ask for his help. The truth was, I found it very difficult to trust people. Then I remembered the dream the Lord had given me— my brother and I on the pier together, and then swimming and laughing in the water. I felt so vulnerable. 'Lord,' I said. 'Will it be different this time?'

But God had been faithful to me. *I can put my trust in God,* I thought. *If he has reassured me through my dream that these things shall come to pass, then I can trust him that he will restore my relation-ship with my brothers and that it will all turn out okay.*

Tentatively I reached out and made the phone call, and by the end, my brother agreed to begin working alongside me to help me get through the tricky stuff. With his lawyer's background, he was the perfect person for the task. He loved me, and God was beginning to heal my wounded heart. Some things take time to heal, but I found that God has been so gentle with me, always taking me at my own pace.

A SPECIAL VISITOR

One Saturday morning, my daughter and I were snuggled up in my double bed together chatting. I had just finished explaining to her about why I had got to the point where I had to leave. That day, she got it, she totally understood, she said, and agreed with my decision. Then she leaned over, looked at me and said, 'Mum I'm really proud of you and what you have done.' At those words, I nearly cried. My daughter understood! God had gone before and prepared her heart, and now, peace filled the room and I could sense the Holy Spirit with us.

Eventually, we got up and I mentioned to my daughter a few jobs that needed doing. 'Would you like to unpack the dishwasher or hang out the laundry?' I asked. My daughter chose the laun-dry, only within a few minutes, she came bounding outside onto the deck, saying she thought she saw me out there at the wash-ing-line with my white dressing gown on but when she got clos-er, she realised it was more of a yellowy, glowing white, and it wasn't me at all, but, in fact, a man—though she couldn't see his face. Instantly, however, she felt safe, and approached him. He was hanging up the washing too, and she began to do the same alongside him. 'He spoke to me,' she said—and then told me about the exchange that had taken place that was not in words, but rather, spirit to spirit.

'What did he say to you?' I asked. 'He said, "let's do life together," she replied, 'and the peace I felt was incredible, like nothing I had ever experienced in my whole life.' I knew at that moment she had met with Jesus, and I remembered the scripture, *Blessed are the pure in heart for they shall see God.*[9] I had prayed for God to comfort my children. Now, my daughter's experience was confirmation to me that God was with us.

THE CALL TO SIMPLICITY

As my life continued to unfold, I came to the place where I knew I was being called back to simplicity—just as I had experienced in the scene in my dream at the home of my pastor's parents. With the move into our cottage in Swanson came a settling in my spirit. A tremendous peace washed over me. I slept for days and days. Finally, there was peace. No more quarrelling, no more discord, no more words of death—only life. This was a new beginning, a new season, with a new 'husband' as God was placed in charge of our lives. The scripture kept running through my mind, *As for me and my house, we will serve the Lord.*

My bedroom in the cottage became my haven and place of comfort. Although the cottage was very small compared to the spacious and somewhat luxurious barn-style home that I had become accustomed to, I felt content. What I didn't realise back then, was that my yearning for space in our home and privacy

---

9   Matthew 5:8

from my neighbours was actually an inner yearning for peace and tranquility, a place where my personal boundaries could not be violated.

Now that we had moved, the relief was instant. I no longer needed or had any desire to acquire things in a materialistic sense. This had never really been a pull for me, to be fair, but I also sensed a new alignment within me. I was now able to live out my personal values fully. The decluttering was cathartic, I was stripping things back to only what was important and necessary both in the physical and in the spiritual sense. God was the head of my home.

HE COVERS ME

After the separation, the cottage became my place of refuge; I felt cocooned in my new home. Thankfully, I carried no shame—only a sense of sadness, as I knew that many people among my circle of friends might never really understand my decision to leave. I cannot say truthfully, however, that I even felt it had been my decision to leave; rather, God had grabbed my attention, and I had simply listened and obeyed, as he gave me dreams and visions and opened the trapdoors that made it possible for me to move away. I felt convicted that I was not to justify myself or my actions during this time. What I was doing was a matter before the Lord, and I knew that one day, when I stood before my Maker and answered to him for my actions, that my conscience was clear.

My reputation took a hammering, however, and yes, people all around me were talking. I was known in the community and was on the Board of Trustees for our kids local high school—at the time, I was boldly plastered over billboards as part of a promotion for the school. During the very time I wished I could remain invisible, I was in people's faces everywhere they went, a reminder of who I was and what I had done. And at times, it was not easy, but I did not respond. I kept quiet. In my dream it had been the scene at the motel that reassured me that my reputation would remain intact. God knew, he saw everything around me, and I felt safeguarded, protected and calm.

The Lord gave me a deep compassion for my husband, and soon I forgave him for all he had done and began to bless him daily in my prayers. My prayer was for God to also bless him with intimacy with the Lord. I prayed he might have eyes to see just what he had done, and that he would slowly and carefully begin the restorative process, entering into a new and loving relationship with his children. Although that was hard for me to pray, as every fibre of my being wanted to protect my children from harm, I had to see him through God's eyes.

Gradually, as I began to see a changed heart in him, and with wisdom and firm boundaries in place, I learned to navigate this tender process one day at a time. I was firm in my conviction that I would never speak out against him, but would remain respectful. What God wanted to work out with my husband was none of my business. It was his own personal journey, not mine.

A SEASON OF HEALING

In the aftermath of the years I had spent with my husband, I was diagnosed with post-traumatic stress, depression and anxiety. Twenty years of managing the situation at home had left me battle weary and completely spent. I experienced night terrors and unwelcome flash backs. Memories came flooding back that could completely destabilised me, sending me to bed for days. I was unable to function, unable to shower and barely able to pull myself out of bed long enough to scrape together a meal for the kids. I would then return back to my bed, my place of solace and rest, my hiding place.

During this time, I continued to work alongside my psychotherapist, who became an absolute life-line, teaching me how to have compassion for myself, explaining what was happening to me, and helping me process each and every trauma that I had walked through in the hope that my past would no longer control my life, but rather, that I could make peace with what had happened and eventually move forward again.

I worked hard at therapy. I journalled, I prayed, and I soaked in the presence of the Lord. On some days all I could manage to do was to listen to worship music, letting it wash over me for hours and hours. Sometimes, God would bring memories back to my mind during this time—painful memories—and then I would release the pain, the memory and all the emotions, laying my heart open as I allowed God's Holy Spirit to come and minister to me and begin his healing work. I used every tool in my belt!

I also started on a course of anti-depressants to sustain me and keep me even-keeled, so that I could function on a day to day basis. I had quickly learned that going through therapy often bought up such strong emotions that it had the potential to completely debilitate me. Therapy sessions left me exhausted, and I would often sleep for most of the next day. It felt like cleaning out a deeply infected wound, painful, but necessary in order to heal. If I buried my painful experiences, I knew it would be like covering up an infected wound—it would only fester over time and become worse. I thank God for professional therapists who walked alongside me and helped me with my process of healing.

As I progressed, I also began to reconnect with my passion for art; it seemed to go hand in hand with worship. I would fixate on certain songs, put them on a loop, and listen to the same song over and over again. It was as if I was meditating on certain lyrics that had struck a chord with me and moved me in my spirit. I could feel a swell coming as new artwork began to burst forth. This was pure joy. I would get so filled with the presence of God as I painted. It felt like his hand was resting on top of mine, that we were playing together, mixing colours, creating, marvelling, and being totally enthralled by the process. I was being filled up and drawn back to one of my first loves.

I often painted outdoors, because it was there that I felt closest to God, the Creator; as I looked around in awe at his wild imagination displayed in nature, it somehow sparked me into action and made me want to create something also, like I was a part of him and had been born to be creative as well. For me, it was never about the end product, but always about the process. I felt like he wanted me to create and play, to have fun and paint for just an audience of one. He and I. It was a very personal experience. He was taking me back, right back, to when I was a child. I began wanting to finger paint, to get my hands into the paint—and when I did, it felt so good! I started to finger-paint trees, the tactile experience and the gooey paint thrilling me. I wanted more. I began to want to dive deep into the canvas and paint larger than life. It was like I needed to have a full immersion experience! I couldn't get enough of it.

After much planning and gathering of resources I was busy priming my four-by-three-meter canvas outside on a friend's farm one sunny day, when my eldest son came past with an amused look on his face. Soon, I figured out why. He was filming me. '. . . and this is my crazy mum,' he said, speaking into his microphone, 'she's going to paint this massive painting.' I looked up and smiled at the camera. 'Hey!' I said, 'do you want to see what my paintbrush is going be?'

Running inside, I slipped on a bright green body suit that covered me from my head right down to my toes, and then jumped out in front of him. 'Me!' I said. 'I am going to be the paintbrush!' My artistic friends had helped me with the set-up, and now I rolled, jumped, slid and attempted to take flying leaps across the canvas, dancing with exhilaration as I totally embraced the moment. I had begun to fully realise who I was in God! And yes, creativity was in my bones!

I love that the word enthusiasm means, 'God in me.' I truly believe that if he places a passion within you, you should pursue that with all that you have. That passion becomes our life source, our witness to others, as they see God in us. We become fully alive to him! I was learning that this was to be a very important wellspring of life and that it needed to be cherished and guarded and kept close to my heart.

The Lord surrounded me during this time, with faithful, kind and loving friends who lavished love on me and reflected the love of God in a tangible and real way. I received so much from them—meals, flowers, financial support, pampering, massages and manicures, practical help around the home, and most importantly, love and acceptance. I kept my circle small, confined to those I could trust. One friend called me regularly and popped around to the house from time to time, keeping a close eye on me. She often received prophetic words and dreams about me that were sent by God to simply encourage me along the way. With her, I could be real and raw, and the unconditional love that I felt from her touched me deeply. As my friends sat with me, prayed, listened, encouraged and sometimes cried alongside me as we journeyed together, I thought, *this is what it looks like to belong to a wider community of believers. This is Christianity! This is the heartbeat of God.*

I was also thankful during this time to receive a sickness benefit from our social security, enabling me to truly find some rest—both physical rest, but also the chance to rest in the Lord. This was not an easy thing for me—I had spent so many years trying to problem solve and draw on all my resources to keep the family afloat and functioning, amidst the traumas that we had journeyed through, that it felt foreign to be in a position where I could finally no longer 'fix' anything.

Despite all my therapy sessions and my sincere efforts to get well again through 'hard work,' I still ended up finally collapsing, hitting 'rock bottom' in every sense of the word. It was a friend who had called in to see how I was, who found me curled up on the couch. 'I'm done,' I whispered. 'I can't do this anymore . . . I can't.' I was pale, my head hung low, and everything around me seemed to slow down. I stared motionlessly in front of me. In that moment, I was without hope. 'I'm done,' I whispered again, then shook my head and shut my eyes. And yet, the scripture in Isaiah 43:2 was still true: *When you go through deep waters, I will be with you. When you go through rivers of difficulty, you will not drown. When you walk through the fire, you will not be burned up; the flames will not consume you.*

My friend took care of me that day. She hugged me and told me I was going to be okay. Then she fed me, rallied those closest to me and put a plan into motion. My mum drove from her city to take care of the kids while I went to stay with a friend, though I still do not remember much of what happened during that time. All I knew was, I had hit rock bottom.

Three weeks passed, and I needed to return to my family, only, I didn't even know if I had the capacity to take care of myself, let alone the kids. 'God,' I prayed, 'give me strength.' That day, I returned to an empty home, feeling relieved, in a way, that the kids were at school for the day and that I could take some time to gather my thoughts before they returned. Sitting down on a chair, I put my feet up and stared out the window. Just then, my phone rang. I picked it up and saw that it was a friend I had not spoken to in quite some time. She did not know how I was, or what I had just been through. But she began to speak.

'Look,' she said. 'I've had you on my heart for quite some time, and my husband and I feel quite strongly to give you some funds. It's God's money really and we just feel like he wants to really bless you with it. Do whatever you want with it. The word I keep getting is that he wants to lavish his love on you.'

I opened up my online bank account after I had finished the call and nearly fell off my chair. It was an extremely lavish gift! Instantly, I knew what I wanted to do with it. I wanted to take the kids away on a holiday—somewhere I had always dreamed of taking them. After all, when was the last time we had simply laughed together?

JOY

And so, we went to Disneyland—and had the most wonderful time! For two full weeks we were together, laughing, marvelling, and bonding with each other again. My heart was full as I ticked one thing after another off my 'bucket list.' We had been so blessed; now I was able to spoil the kids in ways that were, quite simply, wonderful. It was a healing time for them too, as they got to be kids again, and I got to be the parent that took them away and enjoyed watching them smile once more. God knew, that day that I returned home to my little cottage, that I was going to need something to infuse me with hope, something to look forward to, to anticipate and to plan for. Truly, he turned my mourning into joy. I had prayed for strength that day, and within minutes he filled my heart with joy. The words of the scripture were powerfully true, *The joy of the Lord is my strength.*[10]

THE COMMISSIONING

It was clear that God had been moving me through the stages of my seven-part dream. As I watched it unfold in the natural, however, I was in awe. I had passed through the trap doors one by one, and only one scene was left for me to experience—the tea ceremony.

My season of rest and recovery began when God had placed me in an environment that was stripped back, serene and peaceful, like the Japanese room in my dream. He had invited me to partake in the healing sips of tea, and was infusing me with love and strength day by day as I found rest for my weary soul after the weeks and months that had followed my separation.

---

10   Nehemiah 8:10

I began to ask the Lord to show me when it was time to begin writing my story. This was something he had already placed on heart—that I should tell my story in order to encourage others, as well as to speak, witness, and testify of God's miracles and provision, so that others would be drawn to him. I wanted my book to reflect his nature, his goodness and kindness, his power and mercy, and the grace that he longs to give each of us simply because he loves us.

I had tried to write only a month after I had separated, but it felt forced—without the words flowing, I felt the Lord was saying to me, 'Not yet. You are still in a season of rest. It is not time.' On receiving that word, I was finally able to truly rest, not just physically, but mentally and spiritually, until I came to a place where I could switch off my brain from working overtime, and enter into a place where I could just 'be'—calmed and stilled in his presence. Now I experienced pure peace, no striving, no pressure, just accepting and receiving what he had for me. I had finally entered into true rest.

As I began to ponder the words, *His strength is made perfect in my weakness,* I realised that I was right where God wanted me to be. Where I come to the end, he begins. A deep yearning rose within my spirit, as I prayed, *God, I feel like I am running on empty, that I have nothing to give. But I still want to be used by you. If you can use me, Lord, then I want to be used by you. I long for this more than anything. Use everything I've been through for your glory. Let me testify of who you are. Let me brag on you. Send me. I will go wherever you send me.*

The less I became, the more God could be magnified, until it was not me, but him who was working. Finally, I was right where he wanted me to be, totally surrendered, totally humbled and undone. The tea ceremony was about to come to an end. All that was left was for me to be commissioned, just as I had experienced in my dream, to write the story of God's goodness in my life.

Peonies are my favourite flower, and so, just when peonies started coming into season, I asked the owner of my local store if he would order me a bunch of beautiful pastel pink blooms. Day by day, I watched in awe as those flowers unfolded. I was captivated by their beauty, marvelling at how God could create something so exquisite. As they sat on my coffee table, I began to think how precious it was that they were here in my home and that the season for the peonies had arrived. That's when it hit me! My dream, the tea ceremony, and *the peony bloom in my teacup!* I was looking at a symbol. This was the timing of my commissioning; the cloak was being placed around my shoulders was symbolic of his anointing and sending out!

I had entered into a place of rest and peace, received healing in my body, mind and soul, just like in the drinking of the tea, and only after that, was I released to write the book—to wear the cloak. The time right to be sent out to fulfill the calling he had placed on my life. Psalm 118:17 flooded my heart, *I will not die but live, and will proclaim what the Lord has done.*

A LOVE STORY

About a year after the separation, I wrote a song:

> I'm taking higher ground
> In you my hope is found
> I'm not looking back
> Except to see how far I've come.

As I reflect on how far I have come, how far the Lord and I have journeyed through life together, I see that it is really one big love story. I wear a ring full of precious stones that was gifted to me. It reminds me every day just how precious I am to him. I also felt that God wanted to give me a new surname—now, I write my name, Cindy Vida, simply meaning, 'Cindy—tenderly loved by God,' for I am someone who needs to be reminded daily that I am loved by him and very precious to him. These are visual reminders to me.

The passage in Isaiah that has become the key message for my life can be summarised like this: *'Cindy, you are going to travel through some very difficult things, but don't worry because I am going to be with you, and I want you to always remember that you are precious and I love you dearly.'*

> This is what the Lord says, he who created you,
> he who formed you . . .
> Fear not, for I have called you by name.
> Child (**Cindy**), you are mine.
> When you pass through the waters, I will be with you:
> and when you pass through the rivers, they will not
> sweep over you,
> When you walk through the fire, you will not be burned,
> the flames will not set you ablaze,

> for I am the Lord your God,
> the Holy One of Israel, your savior.
> I give Egypt for your ransom, Cush and Seba in your stead.
> Since you are precious and honored in my sight,
> and because **I love you**.[11]

'So, Cindy (for that is the name I called you by as a young girl),' he says to me, 'you are to be known as Cindy (your first name), followed by a lifetime of ups and downs in between (the middle part), but at the end of it all (the symbolic surname, Vida), no matter what you go through, I want you to know that I love you.'

---

11   Isaiah 43

my sonnet

I have travelled through many valleys and climbed mountains too, and this I know—that God is for me and not against me. He loves me with what at times has felt like a fierce love, protecting and covering me at every turn, keeping me safe from harm.

At other times his love has felt gentle, kind and compassionate, and it has permeated my whole being. Sometimes we have delighted in things together with such a joy and awe and wonder I felt like I was sharing a moment with my best friend. At other times he has whispered tenderly in my ear, reminding me how very precious I am to him, like a lover, an intimate exchange taking place that no other could share.

He has always wanted to bless me with the seemingly small and insignificant desires of my heart, and I have felt his love in a way that a father chooses to spoil his child just because he simply can. When my heart has been stirred and challenged to love others better, I have never felt chided, but rather I have felt his reassuring presence steadily and gently encouraging me to take the next courageous steps forward to be a better version of me. During those times he has corrected me out of love because I know it has pained him to see me doing things that are not only hurting others but myself.

At other times I have felt like we were partners with a cause, gaining momentum together as he spurred me into pursuing the things that were close to his heart; I felt his love for me like we were kindred spirits as he delighted in our shared vision . . . like two race horses running side by side.

When I have had no resources left and my heart was truly broken, it was during those times I felt him come alongside me and hold me with no words—just holding me like a father.

Sometimes it felt like Jesus was sitting right beside me, all knowing and all seeing. He knew. He witnessed everything I had ever been through and yes, he also wept alongside me during those hardest of times. My pain was also his pain. Yes, he knew. This love so profound . . . how can one truly express it?

To say that I love God with all that I am is to look back and see his hand on my life, both then and now, in my everyday life. It is to put my hope in him for my future. He is a real and living God and desires to be part of every detail of our lives.

To speak of a God who breathed life into our very existence and our entire universe, his grandeur, his majesty . . . and yet know that same God bends his knee and reaches down to meet with me. He longs for me to know him, to be with him, to have an intimate relationship with him. He changes the way I see the world and transforms my thinking. His love melts my heart.

I yearn for others to know him in the same way. I grieve to think that others don't fully understand that God is not a God of rules but rather our Creator who made us and is intimately connected to us, who longs to draw us close to him so that we may bask in his love and his presence every day of our lives through the good and the bad.

Yes, he knows our name, and he knows us and accepts us unconditionally just as we are. He is love. He calls us. How can we not accept his invitation, to begin a conversation with him? I have learned that he's okay with my questions, my doubts, my frustrations and despair. I don't have to have it all together to be loved by him. I have turned my heart towards him and that is all that matters. We share an intimate exchange. It is not a one-way conversation. He speaks, he listens, he responds. Yes, I have heard the audible voice of God, but the more time I spend with him, the more I have tuned into his gentle voice.

It is a sense, and a knowing, a nudging and prompting.

He leads and I follow.

What a journey.

Prayer of Invitation

God,

I sense you calling me closer to you right now, drawing me into
your presence.

You made me, and so by design we are supposed to be together.
I don't want to do life without you anymore.

I'm sorry that in my attempt to try and live my life my way,
I have done things that have hurt you, hurt others and hurt
myself. I got it wrong and want to be set free. I let it all go
now and walk towards you.

There is a part of me that is aching and longing for more.
Will you come and take my pain away and fill that empty
space up with yourself, Jesus, and be my closest friend?
I want to put my hope and trust in you.

I'm not worthy to be called your child, yet you offer me the
opportunity to have an eternal relationship with you. You died
for me, Jesus. I accept your free gift. I choose to follow you.
Will you come and lead me and fill me with your Holy Spirit?

All I really want is to be loved, and because you are Love,
I choose you today.

Amen

Today God welcomes you with open
arms. He celebrates with you as you have
found your way back to him.

As you begin this new way of living,
I encourage you to ask God to help you
find others who love Jesus. A church
is a good place to start, where you will
find strength, encouragement and love.
We were never designed to do life alone.
There is strength in unity! Bless you as
you begin your amazing new journey.

ALSO BY CINDY VIDA

The Story of Nourish Garden

My vision for Nourish, the community garden, was established, and continued for seven years. During this time, I experienced powerful encounters of the Lord—His majesty and power, his favour, tenderness, and love.

Each page of the book holds a treasure trove of miraculous answers to prayer. Even if you never intend to step foot in a garden, this is a book full of real stories and testimonies to simply share with your children, your friends and your community, along with nuggets of truth that will draw you closer to God. My prayer is that the story of Nourish will spur you on in whatever it is the Lord has placed on your heart to accomplish.

And, for those that have it on their hearts to develop a garden, this book was written to inspire you to see gardening in a somewhat unconventional way, to embrace the wisdom of those who have discovered God's principles for gardening, and to understand that we can ask God to supply all our needs and to see him provide in marvelous ways.

It is my firm conviction that the Lord wants us to develop community gardens that bring Christians together in unity from all different denominations and walks of life to serve one another in love, and beyond, out into our communities.

And by the love that you show one another will others know that you are mine.

John 13:35 (paraphrased)

About the Author

Cindy Vida is an artist and author who lives in West Auckland with her much loved family and cat Milly. She is passionate about the creative arts and enjoys painting, music, nature and the simple things in life.

She loves to share her testimony and explore new places, and is a lover of people and community, but for her there is no place like home. Her favourite moments are those spent in solitude with a coffee in the presence of God.

contactcindyvida@gmail.com

www.cindyvida.co.nz